THE ADAMSKI BOOK OF UFO/UAP DISCLOSURE

EARLY EVIDENCE AND ANSWERS NOW CONFIRMED BY SCIENCE, PHILOSOPHERS, ACTIVISTS, AND THE MILITARY

Gerard Aartsen

The Adamski Book of UFO/UAP Disclosure
Early evidence and answers now confirmed by science, philosophers, activists, and the military.

First published December 2022.
(Revised April 2023)

Published on the occasion of the 70th anniversary of George Adamski's first contact in the desert 1952 - 2022

© Gerard Aartsen, 2022.

COPYRIGHT NOTICE: The photograph of the flying saucer used on the cover (top left), p.15 and p.16 (left), and the one shown in the historical clippings used on p.16 (left) and p.33 (right) are copyrighted materials of George Adamski Foundation LLC of Vista, CA, USA. They are used here for educational purposes in conjunction with recent photographic evidence (the fomer) or in a wider historical context (the latter) that substantiates early UFO disclosure by George Adamski, constituting transformative Fair Use in accordance with Title 17 U.S.C Section 107 of the US Copyright Law, and Article 5 of the European Directive 2001/29/EC.

All rights reserved. No part of this book may be reproduced by any means or in any form whatsoever without written permission from the copyright holder(s), except for brief quotations in book reviews.

The moral right of the author has been asserted.

ISBN-13/EAN-13: 978-90-830336-4-8 (hardcover edition)

Published by BGA Publications, Amsterdam, the Netherlands.
www.bgapublications.nl

DISCLAIMER: The headlines from various media reproduced in this book, identified where possible by their masthead or title logo and graphically edited for space where necessary, are included exclusively for the purpose of illustrating facts, trends and developments in the field of UFO research and disclosure. Their use as illustrations is not meant or intended, and should not be understood or interpreted, as an endorsement of the author's views in any form whatsoever.

Typeset in Cambria and Sans Source.

Cover photograph (top left): © George Adamski Foundation LLC

Cover design: Meryl Tihanyi.

"Perhaps more than any other man, Adamski has helped to keep the subject of 'flying saucers' alive, much to the dissatisfaction of the U.S. government which apparently would just as soon not talk about the things, publicly at least."

John Van Buren
Science writer *Democrat & Chronicle*,
Rochester NY, March 18, 1965

"Time will prove that information given to me and which I have shared with you is true fact."

George Adamski
Letter to co-workers, March 31, 1961

THE ADAMSKI BOOK OF UFO/UAP DISCLOSURE

**George Adamski speaks at the Flying Saucer Forum,
Skyline Lodge, Palomar Mountain, August 7-8, 1954.**
(Image: *O Cruzeiro*/João Martins)

Contents

UFO Disclosure for beginners – and for real   1

Exhibit #1: Photographs   13

Exhibit #2: Physical evidence   23

Exhibit #3: Contact   31

Exhibit #4: Nuclear concerns   41

Exhibit #5: Extraterrestrial life   51

Exhibit #6: Consciousness   59

Exhibit #7: Paradigm shift   69

Bonus material:
We Are Not Alone in the Universe   83

Further reading   111

About the author   112

Acknowledgements

The author is greatly indebted to Marc Gregory for casting his critical eye on the text, and to Meryl Tihanyi for the cover design and her invaluable help with preparing the vintage photographs for publication.

UFO DISCLOSURE FOR BEGINNERS — AND FOR REAL

"I don't believe that it is very important that people be convinced of anything beyond the range of their understanding, for the only substitute for understanding is superstition and where understanding is lacking, superstition always fills the vacuum. The thing we must do is to gradually increase the span of our understanding from where we are now."

–Rolf Alexander M.D.[1]

Where we are now, in 2022, is a world filled with modern-day superstition in the form of conspiracy theories, misinformation or misrepresentation – the direct result of decades of denial, dismissal and derision of the UFO phenomenon by those who didn't understand – or didn't want the public to understand – the significance and implications of the extraterrestrial presence. And in this world, where the superstition that humans have to compete for a place under the sun is kept at the forefront of our daily experience through the commercialization of every aspect of life, those with the most to lose want the Pentagon's admission that it does have evidence of unidentified aerial phenomena presented as confirmation of an 'alien threat'.

Around 1955 Dr Rolf Alexander, famous for his public demonstrations of his psychokinetic ability to break up clouds, had a conversation during which he was told that "the United States authorities had established the fact that flying saucers were manned by visitors from outer space ..."

The report of this meeting in *Flying Saucer Review* (FSR) of March 1956 identified the source initially as a "top ranking American V.I.P. – a man whose name would ring millions of bells throughout the world". Almost a decade later, Dr Alexander allowed the original FSR editor, Derek Dempster, who had become his close friend during his time in England, to disclose that his source was none other than retired US General and former Chief of Staff, former Secretary of State, and former Secretary of Defense George C. Marshall, whose Marshall Plan was instrumental in getting the European continent back on its feet after the devastating destruction of World War 2.[2]

Despite officialdom's refusal to acknowledge the reality of the phenomenon, it has been well

---

1 Letter to Derek Dempster, May 29, 1958, as quoted in *Flying Saucer Review* Vol.11, No.2, March-April 1965, p.9.
2 Referencing the exchange between Dr Alexander and General Marshall in the first volume of his *UFO Encyclopedia*, US writer Jerome Clark claims that the former was an ex-convict whose real name was Allan Alexander Stirling. Unlike Derek Dempster and Dr Alexander, though, Clark does not provide any evidence or cite even an anonymous source for his claim, and ignores the fact that Dempster knew Dr Alexander personally.

documented that General Marshall was not the only official who confirmed his knowledge of the extraterrestrial presence early on, although this rarely happened on the record, and in many cases only became public much later. The Laurance Rockefeller-sponsored Unidentified Flying Objects Briefing Document of 1995 provides some 30 pages of quotations from government and military officials, American astronauts and Soviet kosmonauts, as well as world renowned scientists, all testifying to the reality of the UFO phenomenon.

The document was commissioned to present the best available evidence but except for France and Chili, it had very little impact, even though a copy was sent to the White House Science and Technology advisor Dr. John Gibbons in February 1996, with a cover letter written by Rockefeller urging the Clinton Administration to cooperate with other governments and the United Nations "in making any information they may have available". The press was more interested in the fact that the document was sponsored by a member of the wealthy Rockefeller family than in the compelling evidence it presented.[3]

That same year, 1996, Steve Bassett was the first person in history to register as a UFO disclosure lobbyist with the US Congress in Washington DC. Three years later, in 1999, Steven Greer M.D., founder of the Center for the Study of Extraterrestrial Intelligence (CSETI; 1990), rebranded his Project Starlight as The Disclosure Project. Constitutional attorney Daniel Sheehan, who had served as a Special Counsel to the US Library of Congress' investigation into the existence of extraterrestrial intelligence that had been requested in 1977 by then-president Jimmy Carter, was asked to join the board of The Disclosure Project.

At a press conference with 20 senior military, intelligence, and aerospace whistle blowers the Project launched the global disclosure movement in 2001, "to end UFO secrecy and disclose technologies that would end poverty, climate change, and the use of fossil fuels overnight, and transform every aspect of life on Earth."[4]

In 2013 their combined activism resulted in the Citizen's Hearing on Disclosure held at the National Press Club in Washington DC, where researchers, activists, and military witnesses from ten countries gave testimony to six former members of the US Congress "about events and evidence indicating an extraterrestrial presence engaging the human race".

As noted above, these icons of disclosure activism were not the first to demand official transparency about the extraterrestrial presence that was finally, albeit tentatively, confirmed by the Pentagon in a Congressional hearing on May 17, 2022, the first on the subject since 1968. Well-known earlier advocates include former CIA Director Roscoe H. Hillenkoetter and atmospheric

---

[3] Antonio Huneeus, 'The Rockefeller UFO Briefing Document', September 3, 2010. See: <http://www.openminds.tv/rockefeller-ufo-211/5252>.

[4] Steven Greer (2021), *The Cosmic Hoax: An Exposé*. See: <https://www.youtube.com/watch?v=cGRroNrNGso>.

physicist James E. McDonald. In 1960 Vice Admiral Hillenkoetter stated in the *New York Times*: "It is time for the truth to be brought out in open Congressional hearings ... through official secrecy and ridicule, many citizens are led to believe the unknown flying objects are nonsense ..." And in 1970 Dr McDonald openly criticized US government policy for its denial of the UFO phenomenon, and complained that as a result "nothing resembling any scientific investigation has been going on in the past 15 years".

In the United Kingdom it was Brinsley le Poer Trench, the 8th Earl of Clancarty and one of the founding editors of *Flying Saucer Review*, who in 1979 introduced a serious debate on UFOs in the House of Lords, of which he was a member. Two decades earlier he wrote an essay in which he referenced the findings of the Robertson Panel that had convened at the request of the US Government in 1953. The report concluded that "the saucers were not hostile," but the US Air Force only released it in April 1958, when disinformation had already caused much confusion among the public. If the government had known this for five years, asks le Poer Trench, "why could not the authorities have spent that time educating public opinion to the concept of the space visitors, if they were afraid of breaking the news of their existence at once? All that has happened is that the public have had an extra large dose of horror films, dealing with invasions by Martians armed with death rays."[5]

Officials and the media derided not only those who were willing to take the subject seriously, but even the subject itself. It has been largely due to the efforts of disclosure activists – along with the continued and increased appearance of unexplained and unidentified flying or aerial objects – that the subject of UFOs did not disappear from the public consciousness. And as a result, more research was conducted and more witnesses came forward whose motives or observational abilities were beyond questioning. A minor victory was won in 2020 with the release by the Pentagon of several US Navy videos of unidentified craft that had been leaked to the *New York Times* since 2017, and Congress's implied admission that they are not of terrestrial origin.[6]

Meanwhile, Steve Bassett's Paradigm Research Group (PRG) designated July 8 World Disclosure Day, to "provide a focal point for people and organizations to come together to assert their right to know and demand cosmic truths being withheld from them by their governments". The website that PRG set up for World Disclosure Day defines disclosure as referring "to the formal acknowledgement by world governments of an extraterrestrial presence engaging the

---

5 Brinsley le Poer Trench, 'We Are Not Alone'. In: S.K. Maitra (ed.; 1958), *We Are Not Alone in the Universe*, p.8. See p.83ff in this volume for a facsimile reproduction of this rare publication.

6 Marik von Rennenkampff, 'Congress implies UFOs have non-human origins'. *The Hill*, 22 Aug 2022. See: <https://thehill.com/opinion/national-security/3610916-congress-implies-ufos-have-non-human-origins/>.

human race, but [it] could well refer to a long list of concerns the truths of which still lie behind walls of secrecy."[7]

About disclosure Steven Greer recently pointed out: "A lot of people don't realize the Disclosure Project wasn't done to prove UFOs were real. That evidence was already there. It was to connect all these dots: the technology, the energy, the propulsion, the secret agenda for endless war. That's what the Disclosure Project was about. It's not about saying 'Gee, there's something up in the sky, we don't know what it is.' That's what people think disclosure is in 2021 [as a result of the renewed media attention following the Pentagon release of videos]. But in the 90s and the 2000s we knew that that wasn't the issue. The issue was, what's really behind the secrecy?"[8]

Nowadays Greer is best known for his CE-5 – or Close Encounters of the 5th kind – efforts, claiming contact with extraterrestrial visitors through group meditation directed at summoning the appearance of ET craft. He is also behind several video documentaries aimed at raising public awareness of what governments have been hiding about the ET presence. In his latest, *The Cosmic Hoax*, Greer posits that the Pentagon's official release of videos that were leaked to the *New York Times* in 2017, is part of a disinformation campaign aimed at framing ET visitors as a menacing danger, rather than an honest attempt at opening up about what the government – or rather some secretive agencies within the government – know about the ET presence.

The purpose for this campaign would be for the military-industrial complex to maintain its iron grip on unregulated global markets by extending the 'forever war' against 'threats from space'. After all, these would require advanced weapons for which (more) public funds would need to be diverted into the defence industry. Historically, singling out an enemy (first communists, then terrorists, and now 'aliens') which requires weapons, defence technologies and fuel (fossil or nuclear) has been the go-to playbook for the ruling elite to siphon off public funds to boost their own profits and the power that their riches gives them.

The 'aliens are a threat' angle was already (or rather, again) dangled in front of an eager media – who had thus far largely refused to treat the UFO subject with any degree of sincerity – in the highly anticipated and equally non-revealing Preliminary Assessment from the US Office of the Director of National Intelligence in 2021. While citing limited data and challenges to collection processing or analysis for its failure to positively identify unexplained UAPs, the report doesn't hesitate to label these 'of concern' or outright 'threats to national security'.[9] Indeed, in October 2022 the *Politico* website reported that the American Institute of Aeronautics and Astronautics

---

[7] World Disclosure Day website. See: <http://www.worlddisclosureday.org/>.
[8] Greer (2021), op cit.
[9] Office of the Director of National Intelligence, 'Preliminary Assessment: Unidentified Aerial Phenomena', June 25, 2021.

(AIAA) is bringing together America's top aerospace engineers and scientists "to protect us from UFOs". Quite contrary to the fact that UFOs have never been seen to pose a threat, three committees will "study the technology, how incursions affect pilot and passenger safety, and to coordinate with government agencies and international researchers also focused on the topic."[10]

In response, Steven Greer accuses several of the key individuals involved in the publicity surrounding the acknowledged official interest in UFOs of being agents of disinformation, suggesting that the released videos are of secret military craft and are therefore still not disclosing anything about the actual ET visitors. According to him, former CIA agent Luis Elizondo, *New York Times* journalist Leslie Keane, who first wrote about the Pentagon videos in 2017, documentary maker Jeremy Corbell, and former Deputy Assistant Secretary of Defense for Intelligence Chris Mellon, who initially leaked the videos to the *New York Times*, are merely contributing to the campaign that is meant to instill fear of the visitors.

Daniel Sheehan, who acts as the legal counsel for Elizondo, however, denounces Greer for his condemnation of Elizondo and Mellon, and in turn accuses Greer of misrepresenting his (Sheehan's) statements to promote his own agenda. In his statement, Sheehan says that Elizondo is involved in the effort to move forward "the strategic objective of revealing government information authoritatively verifying: (A) that a significant percentage of the reliably-reported sightings of UFOs over the past decades are, in fact, REAL, PHYSICAL vehicles; and (B) that the "most likely origin of these real UFOs is Extra-Terrestrial."[11]

Amid the continuing official secrecy surrounding the subject it is impossible to determine whether or to what extent some or all of the individuals who contributed to this tentative official disclosure are conscious or unconscious agents of disinformation. With remarkable foresight, George Adamski, who was the first person to speak out about his contacts with extraterrestrials, already diagnosed our present 'post-truth' environment in the 1960s: "There are many phases of truth and there are many phases of God. It all depends on who is promoting what. Even a lie sometimes becomes a truth. What is true to one can be a lie to another. Because of these great differences it can now be said that truth does not prevail in this world any more. Since it is not the truth upon which humanity is founded, suspicion and mistrust are the result. This is the reason why the world is in the state in which we find it today, governments as well as individuals mistrust each other."[12]

---

10 Bryan Bender, 'New territory': America's top aerospace sleuths join UFO hunt'. *Politico*, October 19, 2022. See: <www.politico.com/news/2022/10/19/new-territory-americas-top-aerospace-sleuths-join-ufo-hunt-00062588>.

11 Daniel Sheehan, 'Danny's Public Statement about Lue Elizondo & Chris Mellon' (Facebook post), July 9, 2021. See: <www.facebook.com/danielpetersheehan/posts/dannys-public-statement-about-lue-elizondo-chris-mellonon-april-24th-of-this-yea/1683177385219798/>.

12 George Adamski, 'Real Truth and Superficial Truth', c.1962. As reprinted in Alice B. Pomeroy (ed.; n.d.) *Cosmic Science Letters Written by George Adamski*, p.6.

Although Greer's documentaries are generally informative and well-researched, increasingly there seems to be an underlying effort to elevate him to the status of saviour, for instance when, at the close of *The Cosmic Hoax*, one of the contributors heaps praise on Greer, saying: "Because whoever is out there is depending on him to change the situation."

By all means, let's acknowledge the good work Greer has been doing, but claiming that the fate of our contact with ET visitors depends on this one man?! And while it is true that Greer has been a very visible and tenacious activist for disclosure of the true intentions of the visitors, he is by no means the only one, let alone the Redeemer. No single person can or will be the saviour of the world or humanity, or of open contact with the visitors. Anyone with a healthy sense of self-worth and a modicum of modesty would find it embarrassing to include such an overstatement, however heartfelt, in their own documentary. Critics, though, will likely see it as confirmation of what they perceive as Greer's massive ego.

With the Pentagon's recent admission of the reality of unidentified craft resulting in the first congressional hearing in 54 years, and the media finally willing to treat the subject with more than the usual tongue-in-cheek reporting or outright disdain, the tentative success of their efforts now seems to drive some disclosure advocates to joust for the seat at the head of the table.

Steve Bassett's PRG has a section on its website that is devoted to 'Pre-Disclosure Contact', which it says "is the most difficult and controversial section, but for the contactees the most important". Questions that the section is meant to address are 'How many contactees are there?', 'What have we learned from contactees?', 'Should contactees be compensated for any suffering arising from their contact when the government finally confirms it has known for decades this has been going on?' and 'Should contactees become political, join together and lobby for recognition?'[13] But just as Bassett seems to remain neutral in the spat between Greer and Sheehan, he equally refrains from giving credit where credit is due – the original contactees of the modern era.

Perhaps disclosure activists think their efforts would not have gained the traction that they have if they had referenced the likes of Buck Nelson, Truman Bethurum, Daniel Fry, Howard Menger, and George Adamski, because none of them seems ready to acknowledge that much of what is now being confirmed was already made public by these contactees of the 1950s. Anyone who knows their disclosure business and their classics would be aware of what we have learned from these original contactees, and how they suffered official and public ridicule and humiliation, often at great personal cost. And if we continue to ignore the information that was released through the original contactees, we perpetuate the ignorance that was imposed by the

---

13 See: <paradigmresearchgroup.org/issue/pre-disclosure_contact/>.

Left-to-right: Daniel Fry, George Adamski, Truman Bethurum and Desmond Leslie were speakers at the Flying Saucer Forum, one of the earliest flying saucer conventions, held on the slopes of Palomar Mountain, California, on August 7 and 8, 1954.

(Images: *O Cruzeiro*/João Martins)

disinformation campaign that has been waged since that time.

So, in the interest of Disclosure For Real, the current volume will present evidence to show that the PRG's questions can only be accurately addressed by acknowledging and recognizing the 1950s contactees in general, and George Adamski in particular, as the primary source for precisely the information that has been covered up, dismissed and kept from the general public by authorities, corporate interests, and the media.

As a result, the unidentified 'phenomena' in the air are considered a 'national security issue' by officialdom because, in the words of Jeremy Corbell, "we have machines with extreme capabilities, we've ruled out that it's our black technology, our dark, secret technology, and additionally it's ruled out to a high degree [of certainty] that this is any other technological nation that we know of... we don't know who's operating these craft, who made them, where they're from, and also what the intent is."[14]

The Cosmic Hoax, with its warning against the dangers of the official narrative of ET craft being an unknown presence and a potential threat, shows various newspaper headlines from the early 20th century about unknown craft flying through the skies. Nevertheless, Greer says nothing by way of recognizing the 1950s contactees in his approach. But leaving their pivotal information unacknowledged is a serious shortcoming, since it would provide further historical context for the visitors' intentions and the mechanics of the disinformation campaign. This

---

14 FOX11, 'Special Report: Documentary Filmmaker Jeremy Corbell on UFO Hearing', May 18, 2022. See: <www.youtube.com/watch?v=B1V3B_QenPk>.

makes it all the more mysterious why Greer and his fellow activists completely ignore George Adamski's mission. It is not as if they would risk not being taken seriously, because until the Pentagon's recent admission, no-one who mentioned UFOs was. In that respect, nothing much had changed in the field of mainstream science since Frank B. Salisbury, a professor of plant physiology who worked on NASA experiments to grow terrestrial flora in space, admitted, "any favorable mention of the flying saucers by a scientist amounts to extreme heresy and places the one making the statement in danger of excommunication by the scientific theocracy."[15]

Let us also not forget that the present situation – i.e. the 'alien threat' narrative being openly peddled through disinformation – is first and foremost a reflection of humanity's persistent confusion about itself and its place in the grand scheme of things and our attendant mistrust or fear of 'the other', even as the core message that was relayed via the original contactees focused on humanity's own responsibility in creating the conditions for open contact. Yet, to acknowledge

---

15 As quoted in in John G. Fuller (1974), *Incident at Exeter. Unidentified Flying Objects Over America Now*, p.193.

George Adamski explaining a mothership, with Desmond Leslie supporting the blackboard, at the Flying Saucer Forum convention held at the Skyline Lodge on Palomar Mountain, August 1954.

(Image: *O Cruzeiro*/João Martins)

this, of course, requires an increase in the span of our understanding of these fundamentals.

As George Adamski wrote in a letter to some trusted co-workers in 1961: "Although I believe it may be only a relatively short time before we will have men travelling in space in ships of our own making, I doubt that we will soon be given the whole truth of conditions found. So do not be disturbed by conflicting reports, which will be increasing in number as time passes. Remember how important events have been handled in the past, and take all reports in stride. Time will prove that information given to me and which I have shared with you is true fact."[16]

One reason why the 1950s contactees were effectively declared 'illegal aliens' in the field of 'serious' UFO research was the strongly spiritual character of their message which, more often than not, was expressed in the only terminology they were familiar with, or else interpreted in the only spiritual terminology that critics were familiar with – in both cases, the religious. And as everyone knows, science and religion are mutually exclusive – at least to the fundamentalists on both sides of the aisle. For as Dr Wernher von Braun, the father of rocket science and one of the brains behind the Gemini space project, once lamented: "It is one of the tragedies of our time, that science and religion have become adversaries. Science and religion can be compared to two windows in a house through which we can observe the world around us or our neighbours. (There are other windows to be found in the house: Art, Literature, and History.) Whatever we may see through the windows of this imaginary house, it must fit in with the model of the Universe we have and our place in it."[17]

The quantum revolution is now guiding science to gradually expand its view beyond the strictly material aspect of life, and the fascinating correspondences presented in Exhibit #7 in this volume will reveal that science and religion are merely different approaches to the same fundamental reality.

Full disclosure of the reality of extraterrestrial UFOs/UAPs and their occupants must include the fact that the visitors have been trying to alert us – Earth humanity – to the dangers of nuclear fission technology since the 1950s, as part of a wider mission to bring awareness that Life is continuous and unbroken, and manifests through the evolution of consciousness.

As our expanding consciousness has brought the world together in terms of transportation, and information and communication technology, it is fast becoming clear that we cannot survive our enhanced technological abilities unless we adjust our moral behaviour to an equally enhanced view of ourselves, and seek ways to live as one human family who share the same planetary

---

16 Adamski, Letter to co-workers, March 31, 1961.
17 Wernher von Braun, 'Science and God'. *Jyllands Posten* (Denmark), December 11, 1966. As quoted in Ronald Caswell and Hans C. Petersen (eds.), *UFO Contact*, Vol.2, No.5, June 1967, pp.130-132.

home. Lacking this expanded perspective thus far, our intellect has set us on the path to self-destruction. Confirmed by scores of other contactees, George Adamski's contacts and trailblazing accounts have shown that the visitors are here to encourage us to dispose of our perceived need for competition, based as it is on a false sense of separation, and overcome our fear of 'the other'. It is time to set the record straight, and disclose the answers to the fundamental questions summarized by Steve Bassett, Steven Greer, and Jeremy Corbell (above) that have been known since the 1950s and that can now be correlated with confirmation from various disciplines.

Just as it is not the intention of this book to prove that Adamski had no flaws, never made mistakes or was right about everything, it would be equally pointless to attempt to refute every false allegation, accusation or misrepresentation that have been levelled against him over the decades. But the evidence presented here will show that he was not only correct about the *most fundamental aspects of the UFO phenomenon*, he was also far ahead of his time with regard to his insights into the nature of reality. That said, I will be presenting evidence here and there to disprove some of the commonly held misconceptions about his work, and to waylay unwarranted doubts among readers whose perception may still largely be informed by the prevailing half-truths and whole lies about his case.

While the other contactees of his time mostly concurred with Adamski's information about the extraterrestrial visitors and their intentions[18], this book will show he stands alone not only in terms of the level of accuracy of his information, but also for his depth of understanding, his adherence to the facts as he knew them, the global reach of his mission, and his dedication to broadening humanity's understanding of life and the cosmos.

The evidence compiled in this case file firmly establishes George Adamski as the first in the field to steadfastly educate the public with facts and information that are now being confirmed. So, to paraphrase Dr Greer, we should ask ourselves, "Gee, what's really behind disclosure activists' ignoring of the information that they say they are after, yet has been available since the 1950s and is now being corroborated from various quarters – science, researchers, world developments, and even the Pentagon?"

Because, if the evidence presented here is, in Rolf Alexander's words, beyond the reach of their understanding, there is no reason to expect that activists will understand when official disclosure does happen. Instead, they will just have to take it on the authority of those whose denials and disinformation they have been disputing for decades.

---

18 See e.g. Gerard Aartsen (2015), *Priorities for a Planet in Transition*.

THE EXHIBITS

THE ADAMSKI BOOK OF UFO/UAP DISCLOSURE

EXHIBIT #1: PHOTOGRAPHS

Even as the UFO disclosure community is divided over how to assess the Pentagon's release of videos of unidentified craft, with the subject of UFOs subsequently regaining respectability among politicians and the media, recent developments seem indicative of a tentative move towards greater openness or, in other words, disclosure of sorts.

When the videos were first leaked a *Scientific American* report showed how desperate sceptics in 2018 still were to keep 'aliens' out of their universe, when they suggested that "maybe the tilting, aura-sheathed object was actually a distant conventional aircraft distorted by image-processing firmware and autotracking sensors within the fighter jet's gun camera". After all, didn't a weather balloon cover nicely for the wreckage of a crashed flying saucer near Roswell in June 1947?

To anyone who even cast a furtive glance at the headlines in the past five years, the video still of a confirmed unidentified craft in the cross hairs of a US Navy fighter jet has become as iconic

> **CNN** politics   The Biden Presidency   Facts First   US Elections
>
> ## Defense Department confirms leaked video of unidentified aerial phenomena is real
>
> By Chandelis Duster, CNN
> Updated 0223 GMT (1023 HKT) April 16, 2021

for the official interest in UFOs as George Adamski's 1953 close-ups of a scout ship were for the popular notion of what a UFO looks like. One of his earliest photos however, taken in 1950, shows an uncanny resemblance with the object in one of the videos recorded in 2015 – and released by the US Department of Defense in 2019 – especially when inverted (see pages 14-15). The craft in the videos were also observed by the pilots flying the jets whose on-board cameras captured them, who were genuinely perplexed by their extreme manoeuverability.

In a statement the Department of Defense said: "The aerial phenomena observed in the videos remain characterized as 'unidentified.'" And, crucially, in the wake of these developments, members of the Senate Intelligence Committee now "believe (on a unanimous, bipartisan basis) that some UFOs have non-human origins. After all, why would Congress establish and task a powerful new office with investigating 'non-man-made' UFOs if such objects did not exist? Make no mistake: One branch of the American government implying that UFOs have non-human origins

Video still of a US Navy jet infrared board camera recording from 2015, showing an 'Unidentified Aerial Phenomenon', capable of manoeuvres 'not of this world'.
(Image: Department of Defense/US Navy)

is an explosive development."[1] Earlier NASA administrator Bill Nelson intimated that the UFOs in the Pentagon videos might well be of otherworldly origin.[2]

Intelligence analyses of the reported encounters ruled out highly advanced Chinese or Russian aircraft as possible explanations, and pilots who observed the extraordinary aerial capabilities believed that what they saw was "not from this world".

The *Scientific American* article quoted above concluded with the observations of Stanford University astronomer Bruce Macintosh: "UFO detections have remained marginal for decades; they've just gone from being blurry shapes on film cameras to blurry shapes on the digital infrared sensors of fighter jet gun cameras. This, in spite of the fact that the world's total imaging

---

1 Marik von Rennenkampff, 'Congress implies UFOs have non-human origins'. *The Hill*, August 22, 2022. See: <thehill.com/opinion/national-security/3610916-congress-implies-ufos-have-non-human-origins/>.

2 Pamela Brown, 'NASA Administrator: "Are we alone? Personally I don't think we are"'. CNN Newsroom, June 28, 2021. See: <edition.cnn.com/videos/tv/2021/06/28/nasa-administrator-bill-nelson-classified-ufo-report-newsroom.cnn>).

EXHIBIT #1: PHOTOGRAPHS

I PHOTOGRAPHED SPACE SHIPS

By Prof. George Adamski

Astronomer-philosopher in private Palomar Gardens Observatory reports incredible observations of the heavens.

(*FATE Magazine*, July 1951)

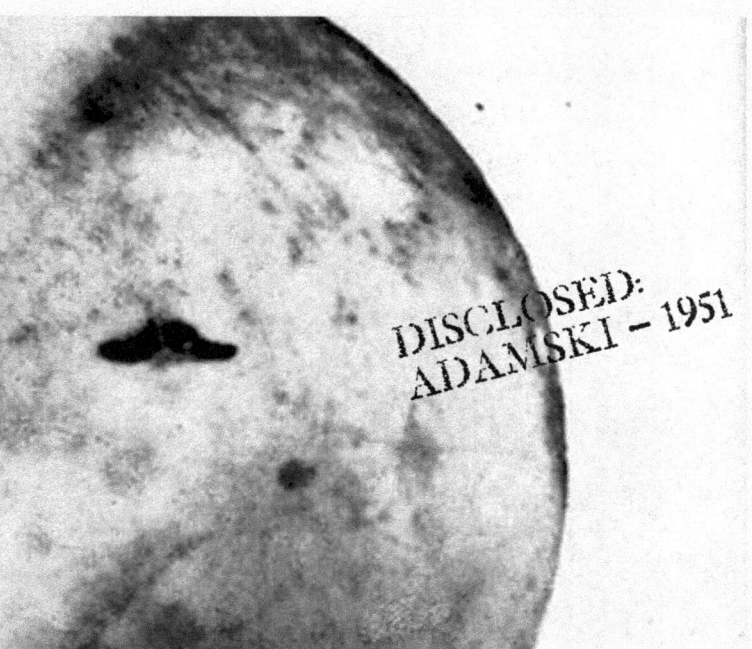

Photo (inverted) of a saucer-shaped object against the Moon, taken by George Adamski on June 6, 1950 (see original on p.22).
Despite the low resolution a faint force field may be observed surrounding the object, just like in the US Navy video still.
(Image: *O Cruzeiro*/George Adamski)

Photo: © George Adamski Foundation LLC, Vista, CA, USA

capacity has expanded by several orders of magnitude in the past 20 years." He adds: "To remain so vexingly residual UFOs would have to become more elusive in lockstep with our increasing ability to detect them – something no natural process would be expected to do." In his opinion, hypothetical aliens with advanced technology could do that, "but then you have to ask why they would choose to remain marginally undetectable rather than just being undetectable. Unless they're taunting us, it's hard to come up with a coherent explanation."[3]

The explanation given in a commentary in *Flying Saucer Review* sounds even more pertinent now than it did in 1956: "One asks why – if such exist and are not hostile – do they not make themselves known widely and forthwith? Why are they so coy and elusive? There may be several reasons: the sudden and irrefutable appearance, on a large scale, of beings of superior

---

[3] Lee Billings, 'It's never aliens – until it is'. *Scientific American*, January 9, 2018. See: <www.scientificamerican.com/article/its-never-aliens-until-it-is/>.

accomplishment could throw governmental authority into confusion, upset values on stock exchanges and generally provoke worldwide resentment – not least on the part of religious denominations faced with the necessity for some fast explaining."[4]

Moreover, if the Stanford astronomer had looked at the history of UFO sightings, he would have known that since the 1950s blurry images and pictures of unexplained glowing lights in the sky have alternated with very clear photographs of saucer-shaped craft. Most notably, of course, it was George Adamski, whose detailed photos taken in December 1953 of what he identified as a Venusian scout ship, have become the instantly recognizable and iconic representation of the phenomenon around the world. The same type of craft was captured on colour film during his stay in Silver Spring, MD, in February 1965.

Not long after Adamski's close-ups of saucer-shaped craft were published, they were denounced as hoaxes because they were so detailed that sceptics couldn't accept they might be authentic, or even that someone had had the privilege of taking such astounding photos of something they had a hard time to accept – an extraterrestrial craft hovering over Earth's surface.

The fiercest early UFO detractor, James Moseley, began his crusade against Adamski in

[4] John Lade, 'Adamski – A Reasoned Support'. *Flying Saucer Review*, Vol.2, No.5, September-October 1956, p.19.

'Which twin is made to look like the original?' – The photo on the left shows the close-up of the scout craft that hovered over the Palomar Gardens premises in December 1953, taken by George Adamski. The photo on the right was made by the editor of *Yankee* magazine, of a model that was *made to look like* the craft in Adamski's photo. Showing that one can make something that resembles something else was then presented as proof that Adamski photographed a model, in support of government denials about events and facts that are being confirmed 70 years on. (Image: *Nexus* newsletter, January 1955)

EXHIBIT #1: PHOTOGRAPHS

the January 1955 issue of his newsletter *Nexus* with an item titled 'Which twin is the phony?' (see page 16). Here he placed one of Adamski's photos next to a photo of a model that was created (by *Yankee* magazine of New Hampshire) to resemble it. In his article Mr Moseley quotes science and science fiction writer Arthur C. Clarke, who said the pictures "seem to be of small objects photographed from very close up and not of a large object seen through a telescope".[5] Yet, fourteen experts of the J. Arthur Rank film distribution company agreed with various other photography experts at the time, and "concluded that the object photographed was either real, or a full scale model".[6]

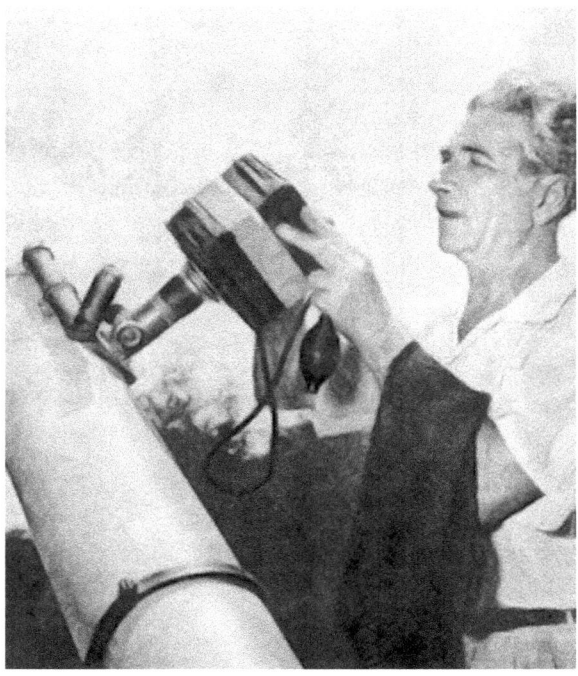

Adamski mounting his lensless box camera onto the 6-inch telescope. (Image: *O Cruzeiro*/João Martins)

Ironically, while unbiased experts at the time agreed that Adamski's photos were authentic, his detractors never managed to agree on exactly what item he allegedly used to 'fake' his photos. A steady stream of 'smoking guns' were 'uncovered' – a street light, the top of an Italian ice machine, or a tobacco humidor, a 1930s lantern, or the top of a chicken brooder – all of which claimed but failed to provide 'definitive proof' of Adamski's supposed fakery. The latest debacle in this regard was the 'discovery' by ufologist Joel Carpenter of the top of a lantern he claimed had been used as the model, which upon closer inspection was shown to be another dud.[7]

One of many other points of contention that Moseley raised against Adamski's account in *Flying Saucers Have Landed*, is an episode in which Adamski describes how four men visited the Palomar Gardens Café in late 1949. Two of these, Joseph Maxfield and Gene Bloom, were from the Point Loma Navy Electronics Laboratory near San Diego. As Adamski recalls it: "They asked me if I would co-operate with them in trying to get photographs of strange craft moving through space, since I had

---

5   James Moseley (ed.), 'Some new facts about Flying Saucers Have Landed'. *Nexus*, January 1955, p.12.
6   Leonard Cramp (1954), *Space, Gravity, and the Flying Saucer*, chapter 15. See <www.the-adamski-case.nl/his-reputation/his-photos/> for a compilation of contemporary expert opinions on Adamski's photos.
7   See Bastien Bouhaniche, 'Rebuttal of the accusations regarding the Coleman lantern fiasco' at the bottom half of this page: <www.adamskifoundation.com/Rene Erik Olsen - Denmark/Rene-Denmark.html>.

smaller instruments than those at the big Observatory. I could manoeuvre mine more easily than those on top could be moved, especially my 6-incher which was without a dome." And during a later visit paid by Mr Bloom, just as George had tuned in to the 4pm news about a flying saucer landing in Mexico City: "He sat down beside me, next to the radio, and told me to be quiet and listen. After it was over, he made an odd remark: 'They did not give all of the truth. There was more than that to it.'"[8]

When Mr Bloom was contacted in 1988 and asked about this passage he stated that he and his colleague Maxfield had only stopped by the café for lunch before going up to the Hale Observatory on Palomar Mountain and he denied having asked Adamski's co-operation in photographing flying saucers: "Everything Adamski wrote about us was fiction, pure fiction".[9]

However, Bloom had earlier been contacted in 1955 by James Moseley, who lists as Bloom's first objection in his "survey of the Adamski tale" that "he has been grossly misquoted in 'Flying Saucers Have Landed'. *In particular, he claimed to have no knowledge whatsoever of a saucer landing in Mexico City."*[10] [Emphasis added; GAa] Is it not interesting that only five years after the episode he primarily objected that he had no knowledge of a UFO landing in Mexico City, rather than denying everything Adamski said? Why did he not denounce the whole episode in response to Moseley's inquiry – when surely he had a much better memory of the event than he did 33 years later?

As an expert from a reputable US Navy laboratory he may have been one of the first, but was certainly not the last who, in the midst of the ongoing ridicule in the media and among scientists, felt they could no longer afford to be associated with flying saucers, let alone Adamski. As it happens, although he did not

---

8   Adamski (1953), *Flying Saucers Have Landed*, pp.175-76.

9   Eric Herr, 'George Adamski: An Historical Note'. *Flying Saucer Review*, Vol.34, No.4, September Quarter, 1989, p.15.

10 Moseley (ed.), op cit, p.11.

George Adamski taking a photo through his 6-inch telescope at Palomar Terraces.
(Image: *O Cruzeiro*/João Martins)

mention a landing, in 1956 General George Marshall as much as confirmed the Mexico UFO sighting saying, "a camera does not become hysterical and that dozens, perhaps hundreds of pictures were taken that day".[11]

Not surprisingly, James Moseley later confessed to himself being a hoaxer who, in collusion with fellow publisher Gray Barker, wrote seven letters on stolen US Government stationary addressed to various well-known people and organisations, "to throw long-term confusion into the UFO field".[12] One of these letters was sent to Adamski in December 1957, purportedly by an R.E. Straith of the "Cultural Exchange Committee" at the State Department. Having no reason to suspect a hoax, or a setup, Adamski accepted the letter as genuine and presented it as evidence of the official knowledge of the reality of flying saucers in his *Cosmic Science* bulletin for members of his international network of contacts, the Get Acquainted Program (GAP). Even as late as 1967, Moseley's accomplice Gray Barker presented the 'Straith letter' in support of Adamski in his commemorative publication, *Gray Barker's Book of Adamski*. When eventually it was shown that there existed no such thing as a "Cultural Exchange Committee", that was firm proof for many detractors that Adamski was a fraud, and it wasn't until after Barker's death that Moseley owned up to being the real hoaxer.

Moseley raised various other objections to Adamski's story and photos, most or all of which have been refuted.[13] Yet, the Wikipedia page about Moseley still hails his contrivance as "the first really serious analytical investigation" of Adamski's claims.

Long before Moseley's admission, George Adamski, who was unaware of Barker's collusion with Moseley, wrote to Barker: ". . . when Mr Moseley visited me, I was able to read him like a book. He is young and is seeking notoriety on sensationalism without firmly adhering to actual fact. He has much to learn along the path of life, and at present he is traveling the rough road of his own choosing."[14] After Moseley published his first attempt to debunk Adamski's photographs in January 1955, in a letter to another correspondent, Adamski repeated his observations: "He is a young snip who has brains which he has never learned to use except toward the distorting of truth."[15]

Another seemingly devastating 'revelation' was to follow. Twenty years after paying Adamski a visit at his Palomar residence in 1958 as a young UFO enthusiast, Ray Stanford alleged in an

---

11 '"Flying Saucers Are Real", U.S. V.I.P. Tells Flying Saucer Review Special Correspondent'. *Flying Saucer Review* Vol.2, No.1, January-February 1956, p.2.

12 Curtis Collins, 'George Adamski, R.E. Straith, and the seven letters of mischief'. James W. Moseley Remembered website, February 10, 2014. See: <www.jimmoseley.com/2014/02/george-adamski-r-e-straith-and-the-seven-letters-of-mischief/>.

13 See e.g. Rene Erik Olsen (2019), *The George Adamski Story – Historical Events of Gigantic Implications*, or Michel Zirger (2018), *Authenticating the George Adamski Case. The Desert Center Investigation*.

14 George Adamski, Letter to Gray Barker, January 3, 1954. Reproduced in Barker (1980), *The Adamski Documents*, Part 1.

15 Adamski, Letter to Laura Mundo, January 4, 1955. Reproduced in Barker (1980), op cit.

interview that Adamski had shown him the models which he used to make his photographs.[16] However, as recently as April 2022 a former associate of his warned: "Stanford has often made statements about some of his own past activities related to UFOs and aliens, and regarding his 20-plus year career as a 'psychic channel,' that range from misleading to utterly and demonstrably false. Therefore, in evaluating any particular Stanford claim regarding a past UFO-alien-related event, it is important to not simply accept the representations of Stanford (or those who repeat what Stanford told them), but to seek out independent sources with knowledge pertinent to the evidence claims, and contemporary documents when possible."[17]

Since George Adamski was at pains to emphasize the physical reality of the ET craft he often spoke out strongly against trance mediums channelling fanciful entities who "are having a heyday leading astray the gullible mediums and their public".[18] Starting at a young age Ray Stanford had a long career as a psychic medium channelling precisely such intangible 'beings', and he may well have taken offence with Adamski's vocal denunciation of his trade, and the latter's evocative photographic evidence. We have to wonder if the claims Stanford made against Adamski were his way of getting his own back.

US researcher William Hamilton III, who gave Ray and his brother a lift to the Palomar Gardens Café and later became a notable UFO researcher himself, made it known that he had no reason to doubt the authenticity of Adamski's photographs: "If Adamski had been constructing small models of his craft, then the large-sized original was making its appearance known in

---

16 Jerome Clark, 'Startling new evidence in the Pascagoula and Adamski Abductions', *UFO Report*, Vol.6, No.2, August 1978, p.72. About the rigour of Clark's research, see also note 2 on page 1.
17 Douglas Dean Johnson, 'Plasma Beam or Fever Dream?' Blog post, April 29, 2022. See: <douglasjohnson.ghost.io/beam-ship-or-bullshit/>.
18 Lou Zinsstag and Timothy Good (1983), *George Adamski – The Untold Story*, p.55.

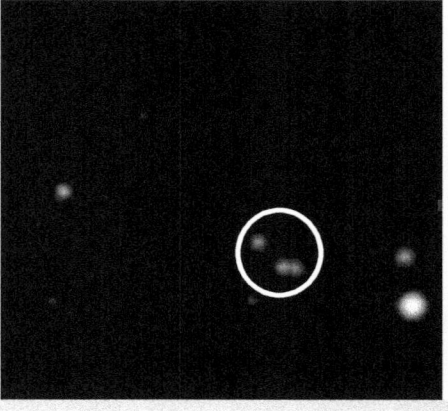

Left: Photo of the sky taken by POSS-1 in 1950, showing lights that were not seen before or after.
Right: Photo of the same area of the sky taken by Pan-STARRS after 2015.
(Image: Beatriz Villarroel et al, Sci. Rep. 11, 2021)

EXHIBIT #1: PHOTOGRAPHS

various parts of the world."[19] Besides, Adamski used a lensless Ihagee-Dresden box camera mounted on his 6-inch telescope to take his photos of space and space craft, which photography experts agreed made it impossible to photograph models or nearby objects.

Now that a strikingly similar object has been recorded with 21st-century technology, with the objects in both takes showing very identical features (pages 14-15), including what looks like a forcefield surrounding it, perhaps scientists and UFO researchers will begin to take Adamski's photos, rather than his detractors, seriously.

Early 2022 *Acta Astronautica*, a scientific journal sponsored by the International Academy of Astronautics, published a paper about a "curious finding" in photographic plates from pre-satellite times that were taken by the Palomar Observatory Sky Survey (POSS) that ran from 1949 until 1958. The paper presents a strategy to identify "Non-Terrestrial Artefacts" that were photographed in or near Earth orbits. It contains several photographs taken with the Panoramic Survey Telescope and Rapid Response System (Pan-STARRS) after 2015 and compares these with photos of space taken earlier, two of which in the 1950s, showing lights ("glints"). The researchers discovered nine such glints in an image of the sky exposed in 1950, and note: "The objects were not visible half an hour earlier, or six days later. Follow-up observations with the 10.4-metre Gran Telescopio Canarias telescope could not link any counterparts to the original transient objects. Based on the time scales and the density of events, the authors ruled out all known astrophysical phenomena such as optical afterglows from gamma ray bursts, microlensing events, asteroids, meteors, variable or flaring stars. Known instrumental issues were also either excluded or deemed highly improbable. The authors concluded that if the detections are real,

---

19 William F. Hamilton III (1993), *Alien Magic*, p.16.

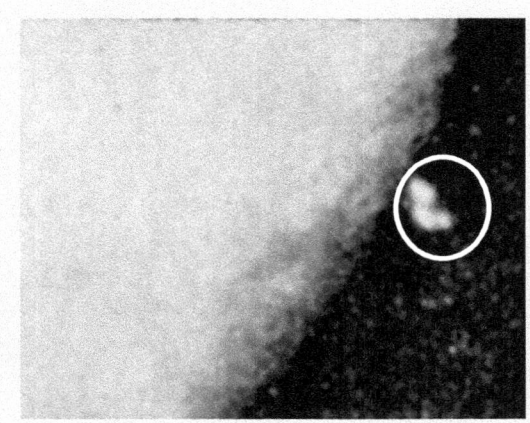

Enhanced detail of a photo of the Moon taken by George Adamski on May 27, 1950 shows a very similar formation of anomalous lights as in the photo taken by POSS-1 (left on page 20). Through his telescope the objects looked and moved like a formation of four space craft.
(Image: *FATE magazine*/George Adamski)

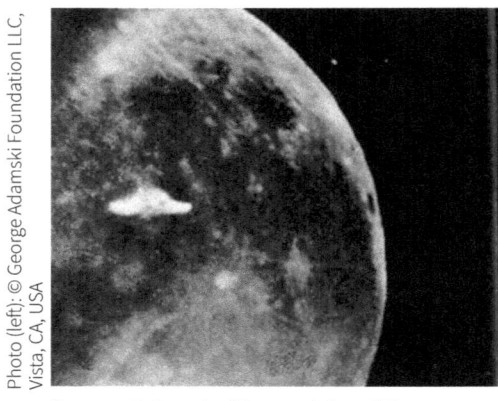

(Image: *O Cruzeiro*/George Adamski)

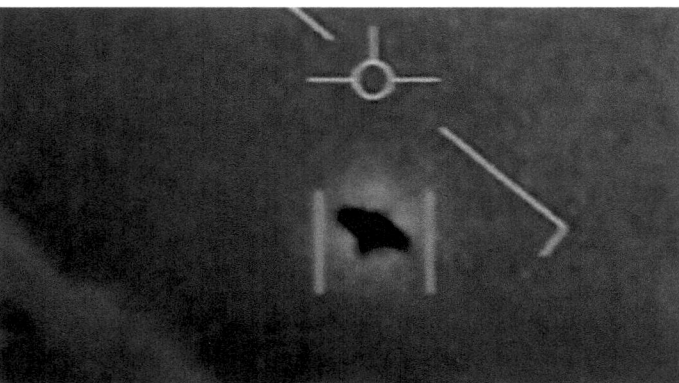

(Image: Department of Defense/US Navy)

According to some detractors the original (non-inverted) photo of the saucer-shaped craft against the Moon (above left) proves that Adamski faked his photos. Because Adamski took his early photos through a telescope, through which the Moon is seen upside down, they argue that the saucer should also be upside down, with the dome at the bottom, to be genuine. That might be true if cosmic space had a top and a bottom, but failing that their argument is tantamount to saying that the video still from the US Navy video (above right) is fake because what looks like the dome should be at the top. Their argument also ignores the 'out of this world' capabilities of the objects as observed by trained pilots all over the world.

then the objects must be located inside the Solar System given their synchronous behaviour."[20]

On this point it is interesting to note that in September 1951 Adamski wrote to a correspondent that the Palomar Observatory had captured space ships in their photos, just as he had: "These are both daytime pictures and night. Some of them were also caught by the telescopes on top [i.e. at the Palomar Observatory] but such information from them cannot be expected, at least at this time. They are working in conjunction with the military and are not free to release any such facts. However, because they did catch some of the same pictures which I got, I had mine copyrighted."[21]

Clearly, the lights in the POSS photo on page 20 show no clear outlines of flying saucers or space craft. Yet it is remarkable that "non-terrestrial artefacts" were captured by the Palomar Observatory, just as George Adamski photographed objects as he saw them moving in space or against the Moon. Also, it is striking that the Palomar Observatory astronomers noted the glints were not visible "half an hour earlier or six days later", but, as Adamski observed, "such information from them can not be expected" because they worked with the military.

Many other examples may be – and have elsewhere been – given that support the authenticity of Adamski's photographs, such as the same type of craft also being captured on cameras in other parts of the world, notably the UK, Italy and South America.

---

20 Beatriz Villarroel et al, 'A glint in the eye: Photographic plate archive searches for non-terrestrial artefacts'. *Acta Astronautica*, Volume 194, 2022, pp.110-111. See: <doi.org/10.1016/j.actaastro.2022.01.039>.

21 Gerard Aartsen (ed.; 2022), *George Adamski – Letters to Emma Martinelli*, p.73.

EXHIBIT #2: PHYSICAL EVIDENCE

In February 2021 headlines appeared claiming that the Pentagon had admitted to be in possession of UFO 'wreckage' materials, including "physical debris recovered by personnel of the Department of Defense as residue, flotsam, shot-off material or crashed material from UAPs or unidentified flying objects".

In response to a Freedom of Information Act (FOIA) request UFO researcher Anthony Bragalia received a 154-page reply, which included reports of materials with, according to Bragalia, "extraordinary capabilities", such as making things invisible or slowing the speed of light, and a 'memory' metal called Nitinol, which returns to its original shape after having been

bent or deformed. Because some portions of the documents had to be redacted, Bragalia says, "They are omitting information on the chemical and elemental composition of the material as well as its origin."[1]

For those who have no time for tabloid newspaper reports about the findings of UFO researchers it is easy to dismiss this sensational news, even if it was picked up by many other media outlets. Such reports, however, will be harder to dismiss knowing that a reputed Stanford professor of pathology has admitted to being involved in testing exactly such materials.

After Dr Garry Nolan had run tests on genetic material from the contentious 'alien mummy' that captivated the world's media in 2017, and found it was a premature human baby with genetic growth deformities[2], he was approached by people in the US government to study and

---

1 Emma Parry, 'Pentagon admits it has been testing wreckage from UFO crashes & findings may "change our lives forever," expert says'. The *U.S. Sun*, February 13, 2021. See: <www.the-sun.com/news/2321251/pentagon-admits-testing-wreckage-ufo-crashes/>.
2 Sanchita Battacharya et al, 'Whole genome-sequencing of Atacama skeleton shows novel mutations linked with

Below: Some of the samples of anomalous material Dr Nolan was asked to analyse.
(Image: *American Alchemy*/Jesse Michels)

do tests on "individuals who they had claimed had gotten close to supposed [ET] craft. This is all alleged, I wasn't there, I'm only the person doing the testing." Some of the individuals he tested were involved with the now famous USS Nimitz event, where pilots and deck personnel had seen anomalous craft doing things that no known terrestrial craft is capable of.

Professor Nolan is a renowned scientist with a number of inventions and patents to his name for hi-tech mass spectrometry equipment. He was asked to analyse UAP materials: "Some of the objects are nondescript, and just lumps of metal. Mostly, there's nothing unusual about them except that everywhere you look in the metal, the composition is different, which is odd. It's what we call inhomogeneous. That's a fancy way of saying 'incompletely mixed.' The common thing about all the materials that I've looked at so far, and there's about a dozen, is that almost none of them are uniform."[3]

In an interview on the *American Alchemy* YouTube channel, Dr Nolan shows some minor samples of materials that were reportedly ejected from UFOs and which he was asked to analyse. Nolan also says he has much bigger parts which he can't show due to national security sensitivities. One of the samples, originating from a well-documented UFO sighting in Brazil in 1957, Dr Nolan found to contain extraordinarily altered isotope ratios of magnesium. He says:

---

dysplasia'. *Genome Research*, May 2018. See: <genome.cshlp.org/content/early/2018/03/21/gr.223693.117>.

3   Thobey Campion, 'Stanford Professor Garry Nolan Is Analyzing Anomalous Materials From UFO Crashes'. *Vice*, December 10, 2021. See: <www.vice.com/en/article/n7nzkq/stanford-professor-garry-nolan-analyzing-anomalous-materials-from-ufo-crashes>.

EXHIBIT #2: PHYSICAL EVIDENCE

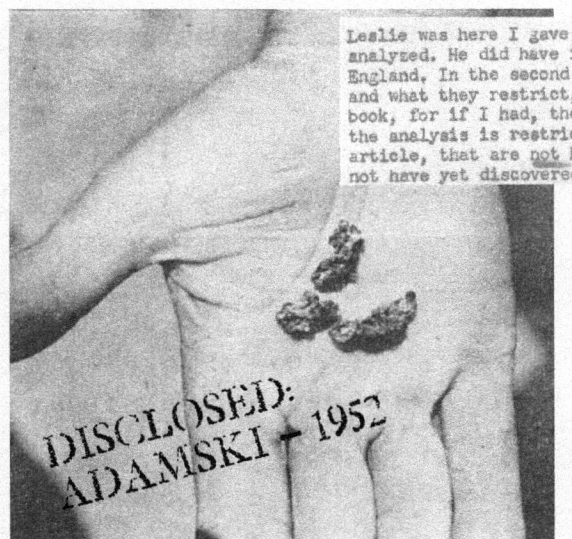

(From: *World of Tomorrow*, 1956)

George Adamski shows pieces of metal slag from a flying saucer.
(Image: *O Cruzeiro*/João Martins)

"There's no metal that people normally make that have some of the mixtures that we've seen."[4]

Former US Senate Majority leader Harry Reid, who introduced the bill that funded the Pentagon's UFO research programme that ran from 2007-2012, confirmed that the government and the private sector had actual materials in their possession. Eric W. Davis, an astrophysicist who worked as a subcontractor and then a consultant for the Pentagon UFO programme since 2007, said that, in some cases, examination of the materials had so far failed to determine their source and led him to conclude: "We couldn't make it ourselves." Mr. Davis, who now works for defence contractor Aerospace Corporation, said he gave a classified briefing to a Defense Department agency as recently as March 2020 about retrievals from "off-world vehicles not made on this earth."[5]

In January 1952, not long before he found fame for his desert encounter with a visitor from space, George Adamski wrote to one of his students: "I have a piece of magnetic turbine which fell out of the sky over Marion, Ohio in 1910. It looks quite crude although it went through terrific heat. I showed this to my visitor [a marine engineer from Alaska] and he immediately recognized it as a part of a turbine out of one type of space ship. He said this particular turbine must have been made in an emergency during flight and it didn't hold up, so was thrown out. He explained that space ship crews can even cast parts while in flight and make any necessary parts to get

---

4   Jesse Michels, 'The Stanford Professor With UFO Crash Parts'. *American Alchemy*, December 10, 2021. See: <www.youtube.com/watch?v=dzTZbSNsKV8>.

5   Ralph Blumenthal and Leslie Keane, 'No Longer in Shadows, Pentagon's U.F.O. Unit Will Make Some Findings Public'. *New York Times*, July 23, 2020. See: <www.nytimes.com/2020/07/23/us/politics/pentagon-ufo-harry-reid-navy.html>.

home to their base where finely precision worked parts are put in to replace the damaged ones." Referencing an article by Kenneth Arnold in the January 1952 issue of *Other Worlds Science Stories*, he adds: "This clarifies the Maury Island and Tacoma mystery of 1947 when metal and slack were dropped out of a space ship into the bay and onto the beach."[6]

In *Flying Saucers Have Landed* Desmond Leslie devoted a brief chapter to debris falling from the sky in connection with heavenly sightings since the 17th century. He documents that the Maury Island incident was the first case in the 20th century where the craft was close enough to be witnessed. Kenneth Arnold, who became famous as the first pilot to report seeing 'flying saucers' while flying over Mount Rainier, Washington state in June 1947, spoke with the Maury incident eyewitnesses for the book that he wrote about his experiences. The eyewitness stated: "On June 21, 1947 in the afternoon about two o'clock, I was patrolling the east bay of Maury Island (. . .) I, as captain, was steering my patrol boat close to the shore of a bay on Maury Island. On board were two crewmen, my fifteen-year-old son and his dog. As I looked up from the wheel on my boat I noticed six very large doughnut-shaped aircraft." According to the captain, one of the objects "began spewing forth what seemed like thousands of newspapers from somewhere on the inside of its center. These newspapers, which turned out to be a white type of very lightweight metal, fluttered to earth".[7]

Very similar pieces of material were found scattered around the site near a ranch in Roswell, New Mexico, where a flying saucer had reportedly crashed late June or early July of 1947. Major Jesse Marcel, who helped with the retrieval of the wreckage, described the extremely thin debris as follows: "It was possible to flex this stuff back and forth, even to wrinkle it, but you could not put a crease in it that would stay, nor could you dent it at all."[8]

An article about the mysterious materials found at Roswell in *The Skeptical Inquirer* in 2017 concluded that the material described "fits the characteristics of aluminized Mylar" and that it was – "although a novelty at the time – purely of terrestrial origin".[9] But that was in the good old days of the cover-up, when Roswell still needed to be solidly denied, before the Pentagon admitted it does have similar materials which it calls 'anomalous', and before they asked Dr Nolan to analyse them . . .

The parts that Dr Nolan did show in the interview referenced above should make sceptics think

---

[6] Gerard Aartsen (ed.; 2022), *George Adamski – Letters to Emma Martinelli*, pp.89-90.
[7] Kenneth Arnold & Ray Palmer (1952), *The Coming of the Saucers*, pp.16-17.
[8] Interview with Major Jesse Marcel in Charles Berlitz and William L. Moore (1980), *The Roswell Incident*. pp. 62–70.
[9] Joe Nickell, 'Roswell UFO 'Strange Metal' Mystery'. *The Skeptical Inquirer*, November 22, 2017. See: <skepticalinquirer.org/newsletter/roswell-ufo-strange-metal-mystery/>.

EXHIBIT #2: PHYSICAL EVIDENCE

On July 8, 1947 the Los Angeles *Herald Express* published an extra edition to report the initial confirmation from the US Army that it had recovered the wreckage of a flying saucer on a ranch near Roswell, New Mexico.

The report in *The Guardian* the next day (right) adds that General Ramey was sent out to retract the initial confirmation, assuring the public that it was just a weather balloon.

A "FLYING SAUCER" FOUND
On Ranch in New Mexico
ROSWELL, NEW MEXICO, JULY 8.
The United States Army Air Force announced here to-night that a "flying saucer" had been found on a ranch near here and was now in the Army's possession.
Lieutenant Warren Haught, public relations officer at Roswell, announced that the disc had been found "some time last week" and had been handed over to the airfield through the co-operation of the sheriff's office. It was inspected at Roswell Army airfield and subsequently sent "to higher authorities." No other details are given.

"LIKE A BOX KITE"
WASHINGTON, JULY 8.
Brigadier General Roger Ramey, commander of the Eighth Air Force, said to-night that a battered object, previously described as a flying disc, found near Roswell, New Mexico, is being sent by air to the United States Army Air Force's research centre in Ohio. He described it as of "flimsy construction, almost like a box kite."—Associated Press.

again about dismissing claims made by George Adamski, who showed similar pieces of slag to a reporter in 1954.

In his talks Adamski regularly referred to the first time he was about to board a flying saucer just as his extraterrestrial contact had been doing a repair job on the craft, from which he had collected a little piece of slag. When he arrived at the craft that was waiting to take him on his first actual trip in space[10], in February 1953, one of the crew members, whom he had given the name of 'Orthon', was just emptying a small crucible in the desert sand, explaining: "As we were coming down a small part of this little ship broke, so I have been making a new one while waiting for you to arrive. The timing was perfect. I was just completing the installation as you drove up." Adamski then stooped to look at the material, "a very small amount of molten metal... Although still warm it was not too hot to be handled, and I carefully wrapped it in my handkerchief. I still have this bit of metal in my possession."[11] When he later contacted a scientist to have the piece analysed, "this man sounded very excited. But when I saw him later in his laboratory, he had drawn himself under control (or someone else had) and tried to brush the whole thing off lightly."[12] Upon analysis it was shown to contain "two types of elements or alloys" unknown on earth, "and the analyses became restricted information".[13]

In reply to a question from an audience member in Detroit in 1955 Adamski explained that although Desmond Leslie had a piece analysed in Great Britain he could not publish the analysis

---

10 Adamski made a clear distinction between his out-of-body experiences as described in *Pioneers of Space* (1949), and his "trips in space craft taken bodily" from 1953 onward. See also pages 67-68.
11 George Adamski (1955), *Inside the Space Ships*, pp.41-42.
12 Adamski, Letter to Charlotte Blodget in: Adamski (1955), op cit, p.18.
13 'Adamski's London Lecture', *Flying Saucer Review*, Vol.5, No.5, September-October 1959, p.24.

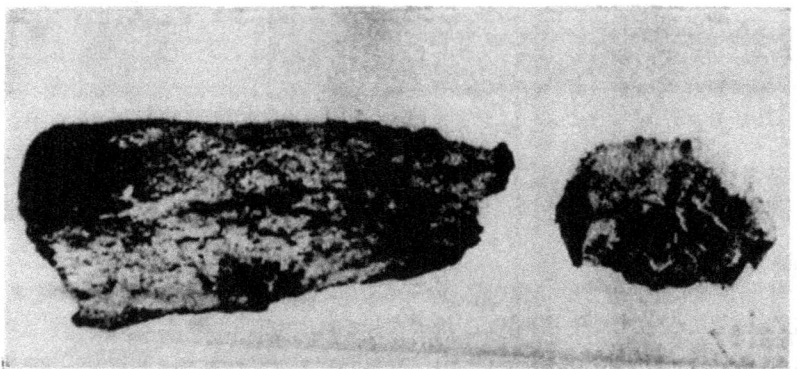

HOW WAS IT MADE?—This is the question posed to the Air Force by spokesmen for the Aerial Phenomena Research Organization of Alamogordo. Tests by their scientific consultants, the APRO says, indicate the bits of metal above were made by no process known on earth. They propose that the metal came from an extraterrestrial space vehicle which crashed into the earth's atmosphere, and challenge the Air Force to join in an investigation to determine the authenticity of the claim.

The slugs of metal from Campinas, Brazil, "made by no process known on earth", that were in the possession of APRO, and which the US Air Force only wanted to accept as evidence "on its own terms".
Clipping from the Alamagordo *Daily News*, March 13, 1960.
(Image: Saturdaynightuforia.com)

because, just as Anthony Bragalia found (page 21), "the British government restricted it and what they restrict, we [the US] restrict . . . The reason the analysis is restricted is that two elements were found . . . that are not known on this earth. Now, they may be here, but we may not have yet discovered them . . ."[14]

In *Flying Saucers Farewell* Adamski references a news report from New Mexico dated March 13, 1960, which stated that the Aerial Phenomena Research Organization (APRO) had notified US Air Force officials in Washington DC about pounds of molten metal that had fallen over Campinas, Brazil in 1953, when "some saucers were hovering over the town in full view of the citizens". Because the Air Force would only agree to accept the evidence on its own terms, enabling them to suppress their findings, APRO declined their offer. Adamski goes on to report that the samples were analyzed by a laboratory in Brazil and an unnamed scientist in the US, and was reported to be either pure tin or magnesium[15], in apparently striking correspondence with Dr Nolan's findings.

Dr Nolan was originally asked to analyse the blood of 100 defence or governmental personnel or people working in the aerospace industry who had gotten close to UAPs and the fields that they generate, because the MRIs of their brains showed "horrible damage". A number of patients were found to suffer symptoms that are now known as 'Havana syndrome', but "that still left individuals who had seen UAPs. They didn't have Havana syndrome. They had a smorgasbord of other symptoms." Although Dr Nolan and his team couldn't conclude much for lack of MRIs or blood samples from before the people involved encountered UAPs, when asked if there exists

---

14 Adamski (1956), 'World of Tomorrow'. Transcript of lecture at the Detroit Institute of Arts, September 20, 1955, p.11.
15 Adamski (1961), *Flying Saucers Farewell*, pp.49-50.

EXHIBIT #2: PHYSICAL EVIDENCE

anything manmade that could have this impact on the brain, he replied: "The only thing I can imagine is you're standing next to an electric transformer that's emitting so much energy that you're basically getting burned inside your body."

This reminds us of Adamski's painful experience on his first physical encounter with a visitor from space in the California desert that took place November 20, 1952. In *Flying Saucers Have Landed* he describes how he got a scare while admiring the hovering saucer up close: "I was absorbed in observing every detail of this strange and beautiful craft as we neared it, and I wondered just how they were managing to keep it in the hovering state as I saw it. My space-companion warned me not to get too close to it and he himself stood a good foot away from it. But I must have stepped just a little closer than he, for as I turned to speak to him, my right shoulder came slightly under the outer edge of the flange and instantly my arm was jerked up, and almost at the same instant thrown back down against my body. The force was so strong that, although I could still move the arm, I had no feeling in it as I stepped clear of the ship."

The man from space was distressed about the accident, but he assured Adamski that the loss of feeling in his arm would disappear in time: "Three months later, his words have been proved true for feeling has returned and only an occasional shooting pain as of a deeply-bruised bone returns to remind me of the incident."[16]

Another instance where Adamski gave evidence of physical phenomena which he observed during his trips in outer space was later confirmed by astronauts. Allow me to quote here from the introduction to my previous book:[17]

During the first American space flight orbiting Earth in February 1962, Mercury 7 astronaut John Glenn reported from his Friendship capsule: "I'm in a big mass of thousands of very small particles that are brilliantly lit up like they're luminescent. They are bright yellowish-green. About the size and intensity of a firefly on a real dark night. I've never seen anything like it."[18] According to astronauts Alan Shepard and Deke Slayton in their book *Moon Shot* (2011), the mystery of the 'fireflies' in space was solved on the next orbital flight when a swarm of 'fireflies' appeared after astronaut Scott Carpenter banged his hand on the inside wall of his Aurora 7 capsule and he concluded the 'fireflies' effect was caused by condensation on the outer wall when he tapped the inside, or when vapor was being vented from the spacecraft.

Remarkably, about his first trip in space – in February 1953 – Adamski writes: "... as I looked

---

16 Desmond Leslie and George Adamski (1953), *Flying Saucers Have Landed*, p.208.
17 Aartsen (ed.; 2022), op cit, pp.9-10.
18 Jay Barbree, 'A glowing mystery surrounds the first American in orbit', NBC News, May 12, 2011. See: <www.nbcnews.com/id/wbna42982294#.WEnkvOErJ0s>.

out I was amazed to see that the background of space is totally dark. Yet there were manifestations taking place all around us, as though billions upon billions of fireflies were flickering everywhere, moving in all directions..."[19]

Elsewhere in *Inside the Space Ships* Adamski describes bands of radiation surrounding the Earth that were only later discovered by astronomers and named the 'Van Allen Belt'. He also reported the space craft he was travelling on entering a glowing patch of light. Similar reports later came from astronauts Walter Schirra and Gordon Cooper during their respective Mercury missions, as well as from Apollo 7 astronaut Walter Cunningham, whose observations were documented in the 1968 Condon Report.[20] [End of quote]

Further notions of conditions in space that Adamski reported before they were generally known occur in a letter to his trusted co-workers about a trip to Venus, where he writes about satellites sending back conflicting data from space. He refers here to the fact that "conditions in space change as they do within our own atmosphere. Such reports, without an understanding of those facts, could be most confusing because they might be in complete contradiction to one another." He stresses that our satellites had not gone far enough out into space to indicate that conditions in space are subject to constant change, just like our weather.[21] Although the term 'space weather' was coined in the beginning of the space age in the late 1950s, it wasn't a familiar concept when Adamski wrote about it in 1961 and according to a paper from 1997 it only "regained popularity in the 1990s along with the belief that space's impact on human systems demanded a more coordinated research and application framework".[22]

Notwithstanding the examples given here, about physical proof Adamski once remarked: "Look what they have said about the space craft photos which show objects *entirely* different from any made on Earth – and which have been photographed by many people in different parts of the world! So, no matter how you look at it, unless the person himself has that something necessary to recognize truth, it would make no difference what was presented as evidence, he still would want concrete proof *to suit his own understanding*, ignoring all the other minds in the world."[23]

---

19 Adamski (1955), op cit, p.76.
20 Edward U. Condon (1968), *Scientific Study of Unidentified Flying Objects*. Funded by the US Air Force, this study is seen as having been instrumental in diminishing the academic interest in UFOs.
21 Adamski, Letter to co-workers, March 31, 1961.
22 *Space Weather: A Research Perspective*. National Research Council. 1997 See: <nap.nationalacademies.org/catalog/12272/space-weather-a-research-perspective>.
23 Adamski, Letter to Charlotte Blodget, op cit, p.17.

EXHIBIT #3: CONTACT

"The UFOs have asked not to publish that they are here, humanity is not ready yet... They have been waiting for humanity to evolve and reach a stage where we will generally understand what space and spaceships are... They, too, are researching and trying to understand the whole fabric of the universe, and they want us as helpers."

Rather than an account from the 1950s, it was Haim Eshed, professor of astrophysics and astronautics who made the global headlines in December 2020 when he, a former director of Israel's space programme no less, opened up about his knowledge of the extraterrestrial presence

on Earth in an interview with *7 Days,* the Shabbat edition of Israel's largest newspaper *Yedioth Aharonoth*.

Well aware of the general attitude towards those who speak openly about the ET presence, he told the reporter: "If I had come up with what I'm saying today five years ago, I would have been hospitalized. Wherever I've gone with this in academia, they've said: the man has lost his mind. Today they're already talking differently. I have nothing to lose. I've received my degrees and awards, I am respected in universities abroad, where the trend is also changing."[1]

Just as it would be foolish to accept everything he shared at face value we would be equally misguided to dismiss the professor's claims wholesale. To do that, we would also have to disregard the very similar statements made eleven years earlier by one of his academic peers. In 2009 it was Bulgarian professor of astrophysics Lachezar Filipov who made the headlines with

---

1 David Israel, 'Former Head of Israel's Space Program: The Aliens Asked Not To Be Revealed, Humanity Not Yet Ready'. *The Jewish Press*, December 5, 2020. See: <www.jewishpress.com/news/media/former-head-of-israels-space-program-the-aliens-asked-not-to-be-revealed-humanity-not-yet-ready/2020/12/05/>.

an interview in the London *Telegraph,* stating: "Aliens from space are already among us, and are watching us all the time. They are not hostile towards us, rather they want to help us but we have not grown enough in order to establish direct contact with them."

Asserting that humanity would be in open contact with the visitors within ten to 15 years, Filipov stated we "were not going to be able to establish contact with the extraterrestrials through radio waves but through the power of thought", and: "Extraterrestrials are critical of the people's amoral behavior referring to the humans' interference in nature's processes."[2]

In an interview via telephone with the *Toronto Star*'s sports columnist (!), Dr Filipov clarified that his statements were the outcome of his research into the answers that he and his colleagues at the Space Research Institute of the Bulgarian Academy of Sciences received to 30 questions they had asked and whose answers came in the form of pictograms in crop circles: "I feel that . . . some kind of information is being taught, that they'd like to be in contact with us". He also indicated that he could not yet be entirely certain of their findings and that he could be mistaken. But, according to the report: "Filipov is no garden-variety crank. He sports an impressive CV: graduate work at Moscow State University, a variety of high-level positions studying astrophysics, work on a MIR spacecraft mission."[3] And while it is perfectly possible that a sports columnist has a deep and sincere interest in the extraterrestrial presence, it doesn't give the impression the *Toronto Star*'s science desk took professor Filipov's revelations very seriously.

---

2 'Aliens "already exist on earth", Bulgarian scientists claim', *The Telegraph*, November 26, 2009. See: <www.telegraph.co.uk/news/worldnews/europe/bulgaria/6650677/Aliens-already-exist-on-earth-Bulgarian-scientists-claim.html>.

3 Cathal Kelly, 'Respected scientist says aliens are among us'. *Toronto Star*, November 27, 2009. See: <www.thestar.com/news/2009/11/27/respected_scientist_says_aliens_are_among_us.html>.

EXHIBIT #3: CONTACT

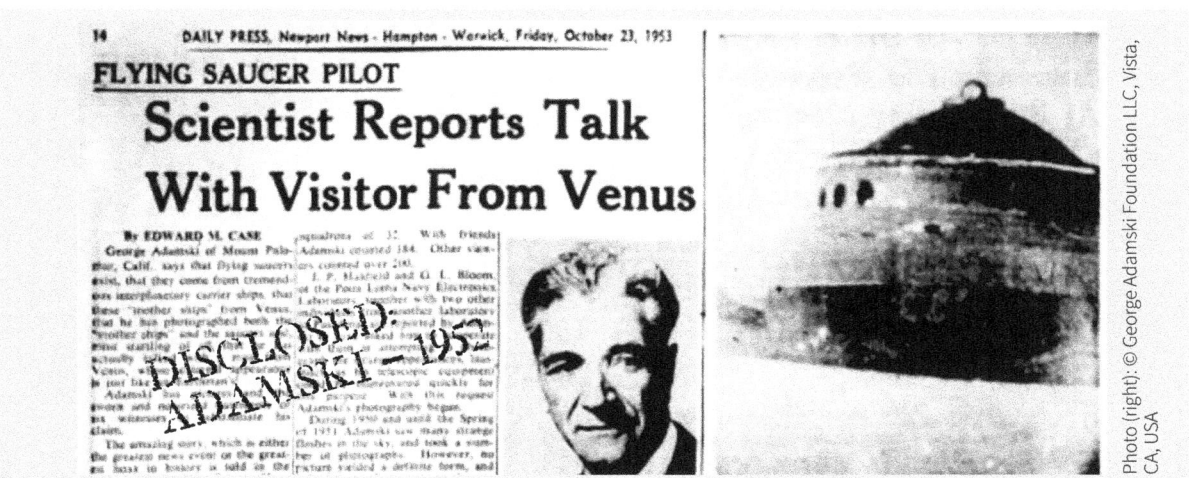

In their report about the publication of *Flying Saucers Have Landed* **the Newport News, VA** *Daily Press* **of October 23, 1953 describes Adamski's first encounter and contact in the desert in November 1952.**
Note: When the account of his contact experience began to be widely reported in 1952 Adamski stopped using the honorary title of 'Professor' that his metaphysics students in Laguna Beach had bestowed on him in the 1930s. Journalists, however, often assumed his residence at Palomar Gardens and his interest in astronomy meant he was associated with the California Institute of Technology's Palomar Observatory, also located on Palomar Mountain, hence the unwarranted qualification of 'scientist' in this headline, as well as various other early newspaper reports and interviews.

Yet, both his and professor Eshed's acknowledgement of the ET presence were echoed in a statement released by Russian Colonel General Leonid Grigorievich Ivashov early 2021, when he said: "... aliens, in one form or another are present on this planet Earth."[4]

Where broader notions align and correspond, they cannot be denounced so readily. Even more so, when they are confirmed by a scientist from another part of the world. In an interview during a conference of the Kunming UFO Research Association in China, also in 2009, its former director Zhang Yifang, who is also professor of physics at Yunnan University, revealed that extraterrestrials are living in Yunnan and Heilongjiang provinces and the Xinjiang Uygur Autonomous Region. In correspondence with similar observations made by inhabitants of mountainous regions in South America, professor Zhang asserts: "Yunnan is a mysterious place, full of oddities. The aliens' intelligence is beyond us. They must have a good reason to choose to stay in Yunnan ... The complicated terrain of these places makes them perfect for observation of us earthlings. I believe they are friendly and they have no intention of attacking us."[5]

---

4 Leonid Grigorievich Ivashov, 'Space is a living environment; there is no threat from ETs or UFOs'. February 26, 2021. See: <peaceinspace.com/2021/03/space-is-a-living-environment-there-is-no-threat-from-ets-or-ufos/>.

5 Lin Meilan, 'Have you seen the saucers?'. *Global Times*, November 9, 2009. See: <www.globaltimes.cn/content/483739.shtml>.

Professor of physics and former astronaut Brian O'Leary concurred in an interview in 2012: "There is abundant evidence that we are being contacted. Civilizations have been monitoring us for a very long time . . ."[6] That his views are shared by several fellow astronauts is well known. For instance, in an interview in 2008 Edgar Mitchell asserted: "We have been visited on this planet and the UFO phenomenon is real, although it's been covered up by governments for quite a long time."[7]

As if foreshadowing the recent acknowledgements from the Pentagon, in a little-known interview from 2008 systems philosopher and, according to a recent PBS documentary, "modern day genius" professor Ervin Laszlo said: "I know that in the US, Washington, the military establishment, the Pentagon, there is serious preparation." Indicating that he knew more than he could share about contact with extraterrestrial visitors, he elaborated: "We don't know the details because they are kept so, so secret but the fact is that there is an entire section of the marines in America who is entrusted with preparing for contact, already has contact and they're preparing for more contact. There are people whose assignment is to do this. All kinds of indirect indications of sightings and, you know, the places where this has happened.

"There are journalists, some of whom I know very well, who are specialized in investigating these things, and entire reports, and details have been circulated, but the actual concrete details are kept very much in a confidential way. So we can't say more about this and also some of the things that I know I'm not supposed to say because they will never tell me anything more. *But I am certain contact has been made.*"[8] [Emphasis added; GAa]

When asked about UFO landings, in the initial report about General George C. Marshall's intimations about his knowledge of the ET presence (see also page 1) he is quoted as saying "that there had actually been contact with the men in the saucers, and that on three occasions there had been landings which had proved disastrous for the occupants. On each of these occasions breathing the heavily oxygenated atmosphere of this Earth had literally incinerated the visitors from within and had burned them to a crisp."[9]

So, in addition to the likes of General Marshall, Vice Admiral Roscoe Hillenkoetter, and the host of other officials who acknowledged, in private or in public, that the visitors from space are real, rather than a figment of the imagination of the gullible, we now have a growing number of scientists admitting to very much the same facts. What is more, these scientists are not merely

---

6   Interview with Brian O'Leary in Steve Gagné, Kimberly Carter Gamble (dir.; 2011), *Thrive: What on Earth will it take?*
7   Interview with Edgar Mitchell on *The Night Before* with Nick Margerisson. Kerrang! Radio, UK, July 23, 2008. See: <www.youtube.com/watch?v=RhNdxdveK7c>.
8   Interview with Ervin Laszlo by Tessa Koop on the *Tessa Koop meets...* interview series on YouTube, spring 2008, which has since been discontinued and taken down.
9   '"Flying Saucers Are Real", U.S. V.I.P. Tells Flying Saucer Review Special Correspondent'. *Flying Saucer Review* Vol.2, No.1, January-February 1956, p.2.

acknowledging the ET presence – several of them are saying that contact has been made. Yet, aside from the instant media furore on the day when these statements were published, no-one in the media thought it opportune to place them in the context of similar statements made earlier by fellow scientists, or by the original contactees. Also, I don't remember seeing anyone in the UFO disclosure community calling out the media for this glaring and seemingly deliberate oversight.

Not surprisingly, the response from the media and politicians has been to ignore the striking correspondences, but anyone interested in true disclosure can't afford to just dismiss the scientists' statements, however unusual, that confirm what has been known or suspected, and carefully covered up, for decades.

Thanks to the renewed interest in the contactees of the 1950s in general, and George Adamski in particular, most readers will be aware of his contact with an occupant of a flying saucer that landed in the California desert on November 20, 1952.

That day, on a hunch, Adamski with six friends and co-workers drove to the Coxcomb Mountains, about 10 miles east of Desert Center, for a picnic and hoping to spot space craft. Shortly after noon they first saw a large cigar-shaped mother craft, which was also reported by a pilot and entered as Special Report #14 in Project Blue Book.[10]

Not long after spotting the large craft the party notices what Adamski calls scout ships. When one of these landed in the foothills, Adamski went over to take a look while his companions stayed by the cars that were parked by the roadside. While looking around for the craft, he soon notices a stranger nearby: "Now, for the first time I fully realised that I was in the presence of a man from space – A HUMAN BEING FROM ANOTHER WORLD ! (. . .) I felt like a little child in the presence of one with great wisdom and much love, and I became very humble within myself . . . for from him was radiating a feeling of infinite understanding and kindness, with supreme humility."[11] The stranger informed Adamski that he and his craft hailed from Venus.

From February 1953 many encounters followed and Adamski was invited on board a scout craft, while his sojourn on a mothership was described in detail in *Inside the Space Ships*. Here he learned that the human form is not unique to Earth and that extraterrestrials have been living amongst our own humanity "since time immemorial".[12] In a letter to co-workers he also described a journey to Venus in December 1960, while in a special report he gave details of attending an

---

10 Project Blue Book was the name under which the US Air Force "systematically studied" UFOs between 1952 and 1969. Also disparagingly known as the 'Society for the Explanation of the Uninvestigated', it is generally seen as an effort to explain away the phenomenon that was being reported by many thousands of eyewitnesses, military personnel included. See: <www.archives.gov/research/military/air-force/ufos>.
11 Desmond Leslie and George Adamski (1953), *Flying Saucers Have Landed*, pp.194-95.
12 George Adamski (1955), *Inside the Space Ships*, p.104.

THE ADAMSKI BOOK OF UFO/UAP DISCLOSURE

George Adamski's account of his first contact in the Californian desert in November 1952 was combined with Desmond Leslie's overview of historical accounts of UFO sightings and ET contact as *Flying Saucers Have Landed*, and was published simultaneously in the UK and the US in 1953. So eager were the public to read his story that the US edition saw twelve reprints in only three years time, while it was also published in at least twelve foreign editions.

However, not having secured an agreement on the royalties, he replied to a questioner: "You'll be surprised to learn I took a loss on my first book." (*Many Mansions*, p.20)

Dutch (1954)

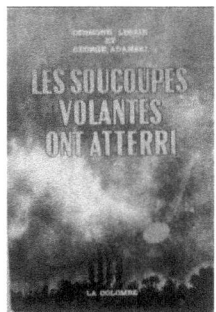
French (1954)

German (1954)

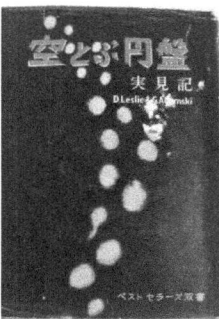
Japanese (1954)

Norwegian (1954)

Portuguese (1954)

Danish (1955)

Hebrew (1955)

Spanish (1955)

Swedish (1957)

Finnish (1962)

Italian (1973)

EXHIBIT #3: CONTACT

interplanetary conference on Saturn in March 1962, which addressed, among other things, the threat of nuclear war on Earth as the standoff between the USA and the Soviet Union over Cuba intensified (see also Exhibit #4: Nuclear concerns).[13]

Although ridiculed by many, some of Adamski's descriptions in his report clearly show this was a deeply spiritual experience for him: "While we on the inside of the ship remained as normal as you are when reading this, our physical bodies experienced a sensation of lightness and a feeling that was indescribable – of eternal well being. There was no awareness of distance away from the earth or strangeness and my mind gave me the sensation of being cared for by delicate hands. Yet I was fully aware of a change taking place within my body and was later informed that the molecules of my body caused the feeling of oneness."[14]

As one of his contacts told Adamski early on: "You are neither the first nor the only man on this world with whom we have talked. There are many others living in different parts of the Earth to whom we have come. Some who have dared to speak of their experiences have been persecuted – a few even unto what you call 'death'. Consequently, many have kept silent."[15]

Perhaps it is worth recalling here that the former leader of Kalmykia and former president of the World Chess Federation (FIDE) Kirsan Ilyumzhinov famously spoke out about his encounter with ET visitors who invited him on board their ship in September 1997: "I did not understand their purpose in picking me up. That is, they did not take me on their interplanetary ship for any special purpose – they just showed it to me. The ship was absolutely enormous. One of its chambers was the size of a large football pitch. (. . .) We landed on one of the planets and picked up some piece of equipment. And they told me everything in detail, the ones who transported me explained things, either the captain of the ship or someone else. I remember that I asked them to take me back to Earth as quickly as possible. Why? Because in two days I had to conduct Youth Government Week, and I repeated this request several times. And then they brought me back, and everything was normal again."[16]

In a later interview about his experience he stated unequivocally: "They are people like us. They have the same mind, the same vision. I talked with them, I understand that we are not alone in this whole world. We are not unique."[17] In the earlier interview on Radio Freedom he confirmed

---

13 Adamski (1962), *Special Report* (Part 1), pp.3-4.
14 While this report caused many Adamski supporters to dissociate themselves from him, 21st-century quantum philosophy, integral theory, and systems science are now expanding our understanding of space, consciousness and matter in ways that bring Adamski's claims into the realm of the possible. See also Exhibit #6: Consciousness.
15 Adamski (1955), op cit, p.40.
16 Karen Agamirov (2001), interview with Kirsan Ilyumzhinov. *Radio Freedom* (Russia), July 22, 2001. See: <www.svoboda.org/a/24197956.html>.
17 Jonah Hull (2007), 'Meet the President – Kirsan Ilyumzhinov'. *Al Jazeera*, July 18, 2007. See: <www.aljazeera.com/

THE ADAMSKI BOOK OF UFO/UAP DISCLOSURE

In *Inside the Space Ships* Adamski gives detailed descriptions of his further encounters with the visitors from space since February 1953. It was published simultaneously in the US and Canada in 1955 (far left), while the UK edition (left) came out in 1956. This book, too, has seen many reprints and foreign translations.

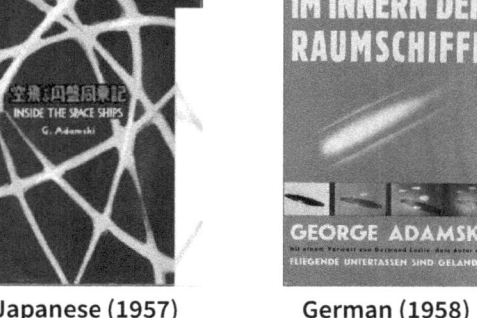

Japanese (1957)   German (1958)   Swedish (1958)   Danish (1960)

Finnish (1962)   Italian (1974)   French (1979)   English/Japan (1980)

Spanish (1984)   Turkish (1987)   Korean (1987)   Czech (1999)

the statements of professors Eshed and Filipov: "... it is possible that it is still not the time for us to meet these extraterrestrial civilizations. (. . .) On the moral plane, we have not yet arrived at a level where we can meet these civilizations, these visitors." Indeed, in another interview, on Russia's 1TV, he elaborated there was a conversation where he asked his extraterrestrial hosts: "Why do you not come on our television channels and say that you are here? And see us, and interact with us? They said that we are not ready for contact."[18]

Adamski's space contacts already indicated why we are not ready for open contact with what by all accounts amount to technologically and morally advanced civilizations: "... man, in his lack of understanding, has destroyed the harmony of his being on your Earth. He dwells in enmity with his neighbor, his mind divided in confusion. Peace he has never known; true beauty he has not seen. No matter how he prides himself on his material achievements, he still lives as a lost soul. (. . .) It is he who fears all things beyond the understanding of his fettered mind. It is he who has denied the hunger of his spirit."[19]

Reminiscent of General Marshall's reference to space visitors having difficulty breathing our terrestrial air (see page 34), in his first interview about his experience, on Radio Freedom, Mr Ilyumzhinov tells about his problems breathing when he had gone on board his hosts' mothership: "We went off to their interplanetary ship, and I started to feel a lack of air, a lack of oxygen. They gave me a spacesuit as well. I did not have time to think that there wasn't enough air, when one of my companions – I don't know what to call him – one of the aliens – pointed to his chest and indicated that the oxygen supply could be regulated by turning a dial. So this is what I did."

So far it is mainly the tabloids that jump on such sensational claims from scientists and others, below even more sensationalist headlines. The serious press, if they do choose to cover it, take their customary wink-wink, nudge-nudge approach. And to be fair, professor Eshed's interview did contain several details that seem outlandish at first, for instance when he seemed to confirm the claims that there exists a 'breakaway society'. This particular conspiracy theory has our terrestrial power elite cavorting in secret collusion with evil aliens in bases on Mars, from where they are running the universe or, in any case, the solar system.

To be sure, the 70-year long official policy of secrecy surrounding the ET presence has provided a fertile ground for conspiracy theories to take hold among the piecemeal bits of fact that have leaked out despite the truth embargo. So we cannot exclude the possibility that even

---

videos/2007/7/18/meet-the-president-kalmykia>.

18 Vladimir Pozner, interview with Kirsan Ilyumzhinov. 1TV (Russia), April 27, 2010. See: <www.1tv.ru/shows/pozner/vypuski/gost-kirsan-ilyumzhinov-pozner-vypusk-ot-27-04-2010>.

19 Adamski (1955), op cit, p.167.

the people who are more informed than the general public have been fed outlandish details, if only for reasons of plausible deniability.

However, much as our tech billionnaires and other members of the economic power elite, tired from coming up with ever more inventive ways of exhausting and polluting our own planet, might fancy the option of retreating to a comfy getaway on Mars, what professor Eshed actually said was: "There's an underground base in the depths of Mars, where their representatives are, and also our American astronauts."

This, of course, sounds incredible enough, but if we accept that extraterrestrials have established underground and underwater bases all over planet Earth[20], that they have been working alongside our scientists for decades[21], and that they have taken contactees, including politicians, on visits to their planets, it would not be entirely unthinkable that on occasion they invite some of our scientists to work on projects on their home planets. Conjecture as this may be, for now, the fact remains that a growing number of scientists are joining officials in confirming the extraterrestrial presence on Earth, substantiating yet another aspect of George Adamski's account.

Underscoring professor Eshed's statement that the extraterrestrials on Earth have asked not to be revealed because mankind is not yet ready, George Adamski said in 1958: "The visitors have made themselves inconspicuous while on Earth, conforming rigidly to our customs; for they are aware many people still find it hard to believe advanced human beings surround us in space. They are cognizant of the ridicule those whom they contact must face . . ."[22]

---

20 Incidentally, it was again George Adamski's information about a possible extraterrestrial base in Australia that, as Timothy Good rightly noted, "pre-dates any publication relating to the existence of alien basis on our planet" (Good, *Alien Base*, p.235). Many reports of such bases have since come out, most notably in Stefano Breccia's account of the Italian Friendship Case in his book *Mass Contacts* (2009).

21 See e.g. Michael Wolf (1996), *The Catchers of Heaven*.

22 Adamski (1958), *Cosmic Science* bulletin Part 3, Question 57.

EXHIBIT #4: NUCLEAR CONCERNS

At the opening of a key nuclear Non-Proliferation Treaty (NPT) conference in New York in August 2022, UN Secretary General António Guterres warned that "humanity is just one misunderstanding, one miscalculation away from nuclear annihilation". And on September 26, 2022 at an event to commemorate the International Day for the Total Elimination of Nuclear Weapons, Mr Guterres reminded world leaders, foreign ministers, other senior government officials and civil society that the Cold War had brought humanity "within minutes of annihilation." Yet decades after it

ended with the fall of the Berlin Wall, "we can hear once again the rattling of nuclear sabres. Let me be clear," he said, "The era of nuclear blackmail must end. The idea that any country could fight and win a nuclear war is deranged. Any use of a nuclear weapon would incite a humanitarian Armageddon. We need to step back."[1]

Twelve years earlier, almost to the day, on September 27, 2010, UFO researcher Robert Hastings and seven former military officers told a press conference at the National Press Club in Washington DC that "this planet is being visited by beings from another world, who, for whatever reason, have taken an interest in the nuclear arms race which began at the end of World War 2." Documenting numerous nuclear missile shutdown incidents that involved UFO sightings, at the press event to announce his documentary *UFOs and Nukes: The Secret Link Revealed* Hastings said, "whoever are aboard these craft are sending a signal to both Washington and Moscow, among others, that we are playing with fire, that the possession and threatened use of nuclear weapons potentially threatens the human race and the integrity of the planetary environment."

At the press conference Mr Hastings stated that the seven officers present were among a group of over 120 active or former US military officials who all had similar experiences. Former

---

[1] 'UN Chief calls for an end to 'nuclear blackmail' and risk of 'humanitarian Armageddon'. *UN News*, September 26, 2022. See: <news.un.org/en/story/2022/09/1127961>.

USAF nuclear missile launch officer Robert Salas, one of those present, said: "Unknown aerial objects have in fact been observed over many of our nuclear weapons bases and other nuclear facilities, and in some cases the appearance of these objects coincided with compromising the operational readiness of our nuclear weapons." He said the extraterrestrials were sending a message, literally shining a light on nuclear weapons: "They could have done a lot more damage, and permanent damage to our weapons systems, and they did not. All of these weapons, in my case, were brought back up alert ... it took a day or so, but everything was fine. If they wanted to destroy them, with all the powers they seem to have, I think they could have done that job, so I personally don't think this was a hostile intent."[2]

In the first report about General George C. Marshall's confirmation, at first anonymous, of the ET presence, the correspondent writes: "... he revealed that it had been established that these were visitors from another planet. That they were completely friendly – their hovering over defence establishments and airports being taken to mean 'We could blow you all to bits at our leisure if we had any evil intent'... and that the United States authorities were completely convinced that Earth had nothing to fear from them. That the USAF had been ordered to take no action against their craft."[3]

Yet, according to constitutional attorney and disclosure advocate Daniel Sheehan in an interview in 2021, the national security state views the UFO phenomenon as a function of a potential adversary, "because that is how they perceive everything. But that doesn't make them a threat. And there's a lot of confusion inside the national security infrastructure right now because obviously this phenomenon 99 per cent of the time is acting in a way that doesn't pose any threat at all. In fact they're acting in a way that's completely contrary to being a threat... But on the

---

2   Robert Hastings, 'UFOs and Nukes' press conference, National Press Club, Washington DC, September 27, 2010. See: <www.youtube.com/watch?v=BtmpaM0Pqyl>.

3   '"Flying Saucers Are Real", U.S. V.I.P. Tells Flying Saucer Review Special Correspondent'. *Flying Saucer Review* Vol.2, No.1, January-February 1956, p.2.

EXHIBIT #4: NUCLEAR CONCERNS

Flying Saucer 'Passenger' Declares A-Bomb Blasts Reason For Visits

By LEN WELCH

Fasten your safety belt, Buster, and take a firm grip on your chair for we are about to take off on a story to end all stories about flying saucers.

Woven into this incredible

fred C. Bailey, 38, of Winslow, for 12 years an employe of the Santa Fe Railway and now "braking" on passenger trains, and Mrs. Bailey.

Williamson's interest in flying saucers was intensified by stories of saucers he uncovered among Indian legends while

(*Phoenix Gazette*, November 24, 1952)

other hand, they have demonstrated – that they can and will shut off all of our missiles [at nuclear weapons sites], all 24 missiles in a given Minuteman silo, which are all independently wired. So they have shown they can do that. Now that, from the point of view of the national security state, freaks them out. Because that is viewed as a hostile threat, which sounds a bit peculiar because to turn off weapons that are a mortal sin to even possess, according to the US Catholic Congress of Bishops and the national Board of Ordained Ministers of the Methodist Church – the mere possession of nuclear weapons is sinful because they're inherently designed to kill civilian populations, and it's a complete violation of the rules of warfare. And yet the United States has them, and they're poised and they're targeted at civilian populations. So if someone were to come and shut them off, who is the violator here? You know, who is the hostile actor here?...

"The problem is that the national security state doesn't view those questions as being relevant to what they're doing. They have too narrow a focus on what the issues are here ... This is a critical point in our history right now if this other possibility [of a friendly ET civilization being behind the UFO/UAP phenomenon] is what's going on here."[4]

Even before his first personal encounter in November 1952, George Adamski wrote to a correspondent: "I believe they did have something to do, from what he [the marine engineer from Alaska who visited Adamski at the Palomar Gardens Café on Thanksgiving Day 1951] told me, with the sudden change in our foreign policy whereby disarmament of the world suddenly became of paramount importance. So that must be their purpose in coming to earth so regularly – he wouldn't tell me much more than that on this particular subject."[5] In an earlier letter Adamski referred to "the constant vigilance of saucers and space ships over military proving grounds".[6]

---

4   Melissa Tittl, 'Declassified: Luis Elizondo's lawyer, Daniel Sheehan, talks disclosure!'. Cosmic Cantina Podcast, June 4, 2021. See: <www.youtube.com/watch?v=QYHctbTnNEA>.

5   Gerard Aartsen (ed., 2022), *George Adamski – Letters to Emma Martinelli*, p.89.

6   Ibidem, p.55.

Five years later, based on contact experiences on twelve different occasions since November 20, 1952, in a letter to Alberto Perego, the diplomat who would soon become his main contact in Italy, Adamski seems to elaborate: "A war could easily break out based on 'separate agreements' between different states and it would be an atomic war: as everyone knows, this would mean the end of our civilization. This would not be the case if a single agreement were reached between all the States. If the truth were known it could be argued that these space visitors already played a role in changing the minds of those waging the war in Korea. Just like the explosive situation in French Indochina could turn into war at any moment, the same goes for the Formosa crisis. We owe them, whoever they are, a debt of gratitude for having extended human life on Earth."[7]

In his talks in Belgium in 1963 Adamski provided details about an extraterrestrial intervention during the Korean War, a proxy war fought between the Soviet Union and the United States from 1950 to 1953. In Adamski's description, the space visitors fired two probes – Adamski used the word "missiles", but they were clearly not fired for offensive purposes – which "came out of a clear blue sky", into the water of Incheon Bay where US destroyers were on stand-by. The impact was so great that the plates on the USS Gardiners Bay were dented to such an extent that the ship had to return to San Diego for repairs. As the probes went into the water, the US fleet immediately surrounded the area to prevent them from escaping but, despite being registered on the radar, the probes came out of water again on the other side of the perimeter.

Adamski also quotes General Douglas MacArthur, who led the US efforts in the war, after "not one inch" had been gained by either party on the frontline, as saying: "We should take the best from each other, like the communists taking some good out of democracy and democracy taking some good out of communism and get together and arm against a space attack". Adamski then asks his audience: "Now why would a man of a rank that high say that, unless he knew what was going on in space, unless he knew that the Korean War was stopped by an intervention from space? (. . .) If it had not happened, you and I might not be sitting here talking together. We would possibly have been wiped out by an atomic bomb."[8]

With regard to the Cuba crisis in 1962, Adamski reportedly traveled to Washington to deliver a message from his extraterrestrial contacts "to an official of our government". Danish co-worker Major Hans C. Petersen, who was stationed at the NATO exchange office there, later revealed Adamski had told him in private that the 'official' was President Kennedy. About this episode, in one of his talks in Belgium, Adamski said in reply to a question why he, an American, should be the only one permitted to inform the world about the ET presence: ". . . there are other contactees

---

7 Adamski, Letter to Alberto Perego, April 20, 1956. Retranslated from the Italian in Alberto Perego (1963), *L'aviazione di altri pianeti opera tra noi: rapporto agli italiani: 1943-1963*, pp.540-41.

8 H.C. Petersen (ed.; 1963), *Report from Europe*, p.120, p.159.

EXHIBIT #4: NUCLEAR CONCERNS

around the world that probably do a better job than I do, but as far as America is concerned, don't forget that there are two ideologies in the world today that could set the world on fire any moment and blow us out of this earth forever, annihilate us with an atomic war. Therefore, we don't know what the other ideology is doing. We in America know what we are doing, and that is probably the reason for me [an American; GAa] being chosen to get the messages through. We do know that the Cuban question could have blown up while we were talking and yet, because of the information that was delivered, we were prepared for and acted in proper time with the blockades, and those [Soviet] missiles [in Cuba] that could have put us into a world war, were completely removed. All because of such a message, which we might say the public knows very little about." He surmises that similar contacts were happening behind the Iron Curtain: "... something must be going on

Showing the massive public interest in the message from space urging humanity to take the path of international co-operation rather than nuclear confrontation, around 4,700 people came to hear George Adamski's talk at the Detroit Masonic Hall on March 28, 1954. (Image: George Adamski Foundation)

there too, because the submission by removing their missiles from Cuba at the time came along with the backing up. That shows that there is something else working all the way through, and we don't really know how many contacts the Russians really had, because they are not telling us anything."⁹

In private, Adamski sometimes divulged a few more details about his covert assignments. In a lecture in 1967 his former Swiss co-worker Lou Zinsstag said: "He once told me when we were alone that he was entrusted with many secrets from both sides of the fence (this was his expression), from the US government as well as from the [Space] Brothers, and this because he never once broke a vow of silence, he would rather play the fool when asked." To this end, she said, he even trained himself to deliberately forget certain names and places. She continues: "I believed what he told me about his entering twice a secret door leading to a side track of the White House just because I had seen him enter another such secret door, the one of the Vatican [in May 1963; GAa]. If the one, why not the other..."¹⁰, ¹¹ Although dismissed by detractors, several sources claim Adamski had a 'Government Ordnance Bureau' ID card, giving him access to military bases, a White House pass, and/or a passport bearing special privileges.¹²

According to Adamski the continuous atom bomb (A-bomb) tests since the 1940s, and later the hydrogen bomb (H-bomb), were one of the main causes of concern for the ET visitors. The initial

---

9   H.C. Petersen (ed.; 1963), op cit, p.130, p.132.
10 Lou Zinsstag, 'On George Adamski'. *Flying Saucer Review* Vol.3, No.5, September 1967, p.137.
11 See Aartsen (2019), 'Vatican visit' at <www.the-adamski-case.nl> for a comprehensive chronology of Adamski's private audience with Pope John XXIII.
12 See Tony Brunt (2010), *George Adamski. The Toughest Job in the World*, p.29, and Jacques Vallée (1979), *Messengers of Deception*, 2008 ed., p.229. *Note*: Vallée dismissed Adamski's case as a "harmless hoax", and – as a true 'messenger of deception' – contributed to his defamation with the unfounded insinuation that he had far-right sympathies pre-WW2. Actual primary source research shows this to be another libellous claim (see Michel Zirger (2017), *"We Are Here!" Visitors Without a Passport*, pp.269-270).

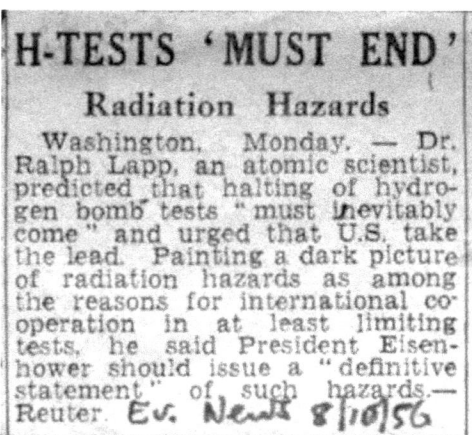

The UK *Evening News* of August 10, 1956 reports a scientist's warning about the dangers of nuclear radiation and his call for international cooperation.

EXHIBIT #4: NUCLEAR CONCERNS

report about his first contact in the desert in 1952 describes how Adamski asked the occupant of the flying saucer: 'What is the purpose of your visits to earth?' The visitor used his arms to indicate mushroom-shaped clouds that are associated with atomic experiments, convincing Adamski that such experiments are responsible for their visits. When Adamski asked, "Why are you concerned about these atomic experiments?", the visitor indicated that radiation from explosions is causing his people some concern and fear that blasts will destroy everything.[13]

Before his first – reported – physical contact, Adamski already seemed to be warning against the dangers of the atom bomb, when he wrote to a student in 1951: ". . . I believe man on earth is playing too much with the universal laboratory of chemistry while he doesn't know enough about it to be given a free hand at it. (. . .) Only something unpleasant in the form will awaken us all to the realization that we had better learn more before playing around too freely in Nature's laboratory of chemistry."[14] And even earlier, in *Pioneers of Space* Adamski quoted a "scientist on the Moon" who said about nuclear power: ". . . what you Earth men have now is dangerous to work with, for you haven't got anything except wild, uncontrolled power."[15]

When the first contacts with extraterrestrial visitors were reported, the world was deeply divided (West vs East) and under severe threat of nuclear annihilation. Most contactees were asked to warn the world of these dangers and to stress the need for worldwide co-operation to avert disaster, along with reported offers to help the world with alternative technology if humanity would abolish nuclear technology. (Adamski's one-time co-author Desmond Leslie was among the early members of the Campaign for Nuclear Disarmament, CND, in the UK. His biographer reports that Leslie "even set up an anti-bomb pirate radio station run by Bertrand Russell and Vanessa Redgrave" on the roof of his flat in St John's Wood, London.[16]) Being gravely concerned about the massive public interest in this hopeful message of international brotherhood and peace, the political, military and corporate establishments started a concerted disinformation campaign to scare and confuse the public about the extraterrestrial visitors.[17]

During his first reported sojourn on a mothership in 1953 Adamski was told: ". . . our main purpose in coming to you [the Earth] at this time is to warn you of the grave danger which threatens men of Earth today. (. . .) Even though the power and radiation from the test explosions have not yet gone out beyond your Earth's sphere of influence, these radiations are endangering

---

13 Len Welch, 'Flying Saucer 'Passenger' Declares A-Bomb Blasts Reason for Visits'. *Phoenix Gazette*, November 24, 1952.
14 Aartsen (2022), op cit, p.59.
15 Adamski (1949), *Pioneers of Space*, pp.84-85.
16 Robert O'Byrne (2010), *Desmond Leslie (1921-2001) – The Biography of an Irish Gentleman*, p.102.
17 See e.g. Aartsen (2011), *Here to Help: UFOs and the Space Brothers*, Chapter 2; or Aartsen (2016), *Before Disclosure – Dispelling the fog of speculation*, Chapter 1.

the life of men on Earth. A decomposition will set in that, in time, will fill your atmosphere with the deadly elements which your scientists and your military men have confined into what you term 'bombs'... If (...) mankind on Earth should release such power against one another in full warfare, a large part of Earth's population could be annihilated, your soil rendered sterile, your water poisoned and barren to life for many years to come. It is possible that the body of your planet itself could be mutilated to an extent that would destroy her balance in our galaxy. (...) For us, traveling through space could be made difficult and dangerous for a long time to come, since the energies released in such multiple explosions would then penetrate through your atmosphere into outer space."[18]

When Adamski asked the visitors if the drastic changes in the atmospheric conditions of Earth could be the result of the nuclear tests, the reply was: "They have indeed! And we are not guessing. Our instruments have registered those results. We KNOW!"[19] Such abnormal conditions build up within the ionosphere through the explosion of nuclear devices. "As a result, our atmosphere is being polluted (...) by the nuclear bombs that have been, and are still being, exploded around the world. This is an abnormal condition of our own making (...) only we can change it."[20] One of the dangerous conditions that arise from nuclear tests, according to Adamski, are concentrations of radiation which at times gather together and under certain circumstances "can extract enough elements from the atmosphere as 'fireballs'. With their finer instruments, space people are able to detect these (...) pockets of radiation, visible or invisible; and when they do, they intercept and disintegrate them..."[21]

In his letter to consul Perego, Adamski explains: "You ask me the reason for the explosions. – It is known in scientific circles that in the thin layer of our atmosphere remain, here and there, residues of atomic energy as a result of experiments with thermonuclear bombs. When the inhabitants of other planets pass through these concentrations with their aircraft, which have not yet exploded due to natural circumstances, they cause them to explode and thus nullify the danger."[22]

Similarly, "atomic clouds that result from atomic explosions are composed of the same concentrated energy, but on a much larger scale. When an airplane flies into such a cloud it would either explode or disintegrate. With their more sophisticated instruments the Space Brothers can detect and neutralize these clouds of destruction."[23] And without their intervention, said

---

18 Adamski (1955), *Inside the Space Ships*, pp.91-92.
19 Ibid., p.98.
20 Adamski (1958), *Cosmic Science* bulletin, Part 4, Question 73.
21 Ibid, Part 2, Question 27.
22 Adamski, Letter to Alberto Perego, op cit.
23 Adamski (1958), op cit, Part 2, Question 28.

EXHIBIT #4: NUCLEAR CONCERNS

'Good Defeats Evil'. This allegorical sculpture created from fragments of decommissioned Soviet SS-20 and United States Pershing nuclear missiles, located at the UN Headquarters in New York, depicts St George slaying a double-headed dragon as a symbol of nuclear war averted by historic treaties between the Soviet Union and United States. St George was a third century saint whose feast day is celebrated on April 23, which is also the day George Adamski died of heart failure in 1965. (Image: UN/Ingrid Kasper)

Adamski, the radiation would "be much more pervasive than it is today".[24]

Recently, at the request of the Peace in Space project founded and run by Carol Rosin, who was Wernher von Braun's spokesperson at the end of his life, Russian Colonel General Leonid Grigorievich Ivashov gave a poignant statement against the weaponization of space. Ivashov is not only president of the Russian Academy of Geopolitical Problems, doctor of Historical Sciences and professor, but also an honorary scientific expert of the Ecology of the Unknown Association. He states unequivocally: "Why do I believe that this threat can be, and is the most important, the most crucial threat to the life of humanity today? Because, first of all, space is a living environment. It is not some dead emptiness which is usually spoken of. But there exist in space other life forms.

"And this has been proven by both Russian and foreign thinkers, including academician Vernadsky, academician Kaznacheyev, expert Kpzyrev and others. Here, we are living on planet Earth. We are part of this large living system, the Universe. And, therefore, any invasion of space, especially for the purpose of placing, testing and using new weapons, new types of weapons, not just weapons of mass destruction, but far superior ones in their lethal effectiveness to nuclear weapons that pose a threat to humanity."

When Colonel Ivashov acknowledges the extraterrestrial presence on Earth, he assures us:

---
24 Ibid., Part 2, Question 26.

"... so far, the extraterrestrials have not caused any damage with their presence – no damage to earthlings, infrastructure, or any other living organism on Earth. So to say there is an alien threat, well, that probability doesn't correspond to reality. And if other extraterrestrial civilizations have contact with the Earth, they are more developed than we are. And they are educated. And they understand that in any living system, especially in the system of the Universe, in the system of universal civilizations, you cannot damage another element of this life without destroying this system as a whole."[25]

In addition to the obvious destruction caused by nuclear bombs, the storing of nuclear waste and the continued testing and implementation of nuclear fission reactions for new weaponry and in nuclear power plants causes damage that is as harmful as it is invisible. This was confirmed by participants in the Italian Amicizia or Friendship Case of contact between extraterrestrials and over a hundred Italians that started in 1956.

In an interview with Italian weekly *Le Ore*, that was translated for *Flying Saucer Review*, journalist Bruno Ghibaudi, who was one of the members of the Italian group of contactees, confirmed: "What is happening now is simply that the infant civilization of Earth-Man being at a point of particularly grave crisis, the space beings are prepared to reveal themselves to us more. Ghibaudi confirms, then, their benevolence and their desire to help us. (. . .) Their aim is to prevent nuclear disaster." Gordon Creighton, who translated the interview, writes: "Ghibaudi says flatly that they have indicated their firm intention to intervene if it becomes unavoidable."[26]

Describing some of the extraterrestrials that the Friendship group had contact with, Alberto Perego, who was also a member of the group, wrote in one of his books: "We must be grateful to them for the permanent dredging of our atmosphere, which, without them, would have already been irreparably contaminated by residues of our atomic explosions. We must be grateful to them for having prevented, until now, nuclear war."[27]

---

25 Leonid Grigorievich Ivashov, 'Space is a living environment; there is no threat from ETs or UFOs'. February 26, 2021. See: <peaceinspace.com/2021/03/space-is-a-living-environment-there-is-no-threat-from-ets-or-ufos/>.
26 Gordon W. Creighton, 'The Italian Scene – Part 3: Bruno Ghibaudi's contact claim'. *Flying Saucer Review* Vol.9, No.3, May-June 1963, p.19.
27 Perego (1963), op cit, pp.532-34.

EXHIBIT #5: EXTRATERRESTRIAL LIFE

It is one thing to claim that UFOs are of extraterrestrial origin, but it is still quite a jump to then maintain that these craft originate from planets in our own solar system. And this, of course, is where proper scientists will decide that Adamski and the other contactees were either fantasists or deluded.

Evidently, none of the scientists quoted in the preceding pages claim that the ET visitors on Earth are from Venus or anywhere else nearby. As recently as 2011 Dr Howard Smith, a senior astrophysicist at Harvard University, said: "We have found that most other planets and solar

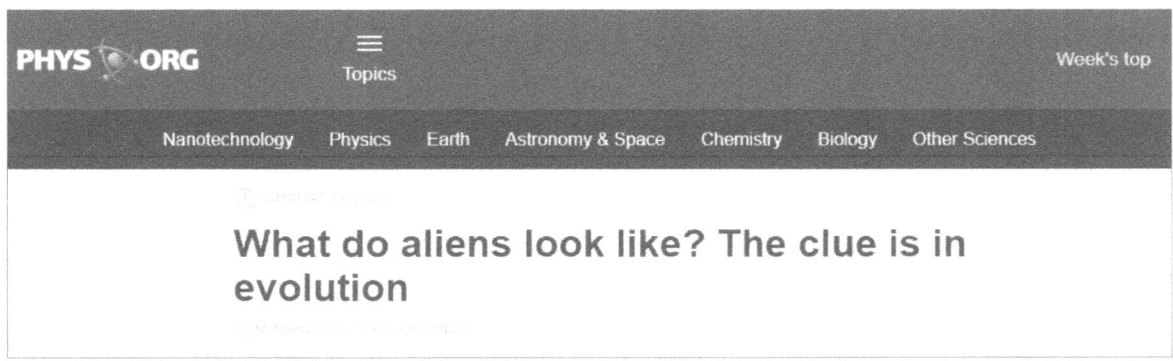

systems are wildly different from our own. They are very hostile to life as we know it, which suggests we could effectively be alone in the universe."[1]

However, in his first account about meeting a man from space, George Adamski observes: "Despite the conclusions of most 'orthodox' scientists it has always seemed to me a fallacy to believe that other planets are not the home of intelligent beings even as is our Earth."[2] And as early as 1960, Russian biologist Yuri Rall concluded from his research that there may be life on 150,000 planets. Also, he disagreed with science-fiction writers who depict intelligent extraterrestrial life as utterly unlike humans: "The law of unity of physiological functions and the most economical adaptation to environment must inevitably lead to a similarity in principle of the higher organisms in the universe."[3] This view is now known as 'evolutionary convergence'

---

1   Maria Court, 'Harvard boffin skeptical over extraterrestrial sightings'. Bournemouth *Daily Echo*, January 29, 2011. See: <www.bournemouthecho.co.uk/news/8820628.harvard-boffin-sceptical-over-extra-terrestrial-sightings/>.
2   Desmond Leslie and George Adamski (1953), *Flying Saucers Have Landed*, p.203.
3   'Human life on 150,000 planets – Russian biologists bold claim'. *Flying Saucer Review* Vol.6, No.5, September-October 1960, p.9.

and in recent years has been gaining ground among evolutionary biologists.

Indeed, the latest insights and findings of astrobiology strongly suggest that life is a universal occurrence, which I summarized in *UFOs and the Pioneers of Oneness* as follows:

Just looking at the latest findings from science itself, life seems rather more abundant than it is generally given credit for. For instance, based on recent research astrobiologists have shown that "if the origin of life can occur rather easily, we should live in a cosmic zoo, as the innovations necessary to lead to complex life will occur with high probability given sufficient time and habitat. On the other hand, if the origin of life is rare, then we might live in a rather empty universe."[4]

Separate findings imply that life is more likely the rule than the exception in the universe. 3.7 Billion-year-old fossils of microorganisms indicate that life originated more than four billion years ago in the Hadean eon, before the earliest rocks were formed, while Earth itself only formed 0.9 billion years prior. Dr Abigail Allwood, of NASA's Jet Propulsion Laboratory, concluded: "Give life half an opportunity and it'll run with it. Our understanding of the nature of life in the Universe is shaped by how long it took for Earth to establish the planetary conditions for life. If life could find a foothold here, and leave such an imprint that vestiges exist even though only a minuscule sliver of metamorphic rock is all that remains from that time, then life is not a fussy, reluctant and unlikely thing. Suddenly, Mars may look even more promising than before as a potential abode for past life."[5]

Dr Allwood's conclusion recently found support in a research paper by David Kipping, assistant professor in Columbia University's Department of Astronomy, who used a statistical technique to shed light on how complex extraterrestrial life might evolve on other worlds. While he says his analysis cannot provide certainties or guarantees, "the case for a universe teeming with life emerges

---

4   William Bains and Dirk Schulze-Makuch, 'The (Near) Inevitability of the Evolution of Complex, Macroscopic Life'. MDPI, 30 June 2016. See: <www.mdpi.com/2075-1729/6/3/25/htm>.

5   Ian Johnston, 'World's oldest fossils found in discovery with 'staggering' implications for search for alien life'. *The Independent*, 31 August 2016. See: <www.independent.co.uk/news/science/oldest-fossils-world-alien-life-earth-mars-greenland-a7218191.html>.

EXHIBIT #5: EXTRATERRESTRIAL LIFE

HUMAN BEINGS EXIST THROUGHOUT THE UNIVERSE

By GEORGE ADAMSKI

DISCLOSED: ADAMSKI – 1955

It is now five years since my momentous first meeting... of humanity throughout the universe. The rich man, the poor man, are equally holy...

as the favored bet."[6] [End of quote]

Not only does science now begin to accept that life is far more common in the Universe than previously thought, but where it occurs a growing number of astrobiologists find that it will almost inevitably evolve along similar lines as it has on Earth, with the human form a strong possibility of being the outcome.[7] For many years, the idea that human-like life forms would have evolved elsewhere in the Universe was deemed by scientists naïve and anthropocentric, to put it mildly. But this is no longer the only view held in circles of evolutionary biologists.

One proponent of evolutionary convergence – the notion that evolutionary outcomes are more predictable than random – is University of Cambridge professor of palaeobiology Simon Conway Morris. Although in 2011 he still expressed his doubts about the existence of extraterrestrials, "because it is unthinkable that advanced space travellers should not have reached the Earth by now"[8], based on his research into evolutionary biology in late 2021 he asserts: "One can say with reasonable confidence that the likelihood of something analogous to a human evolving is really pretty high. And given the number of potential planets that we now have good reason to think exist, even if the dice only come up the right way every 1 in 100 throws, that still leads to a very large number of intelligences scattered around, that are likely to be similar to us."[9]

In *Inside the Space Ships* Adamski describes his first physical journey into outer space on board a Venusian scout craft that takes him to its mothership. Once there he is informed: "The first fact your people must realize is that the inhabitants of other worlds are not fundamentally different

---

6   David Kipping, 'An objective Bayesian analysis of life's early start and our late arrival'. Proceeding of the National Academy of Sciences, 18 May 2020. See: <www.pnas.org/content/early/2020/05/12/1921655117>.
7   Matthew Wills, 'What do aliens look like? The clue is in evolution'. Phys.org, August 19, 2016. See: <phys.org/news/2016-08-aliens-clue-evolution.html>.
8   Court (2011), op cit.
9   Paul Parsons, 'Could humans be the dominant species in the Universe, and we just don't know it yet?'. *BBC Science Focus*, November 19, 2021. See: <www.sciencefocus.com/space/science-of-dune-humans-evolve/>.

from Earth men. The purpose of life on other worlds is basically the same as yours. Inherent in all mankind, however deeply buried it may be, is the yearning to rise to something higher."[10] On this occasion he was also told: ". . . when the book on which you are now working reaches the public, the story of your first contact out on the desert with our Brother from the planet which you call Venus will encourage others from many countries to write you of their experiences."[11]

Earlier, during his out-of-body experiences described in *Pioneers of Space*, Adamski was told

---

10 George Adamski (1955), *Inside the Space Ships*, p.88.
11 Ibidem, p.40.

George Adamski's main contact in Italy, Dr Alberto Perego, who was also a protagonist in the Italian Friendship case of ET contact, included photos of the pilot of a UFO in two of his books. Describing the pilot, he says: "Let's look at the photographs of a real extraterrestrial pilot (taken in Italy in 1957)… We see in fact a man with glasses, his mouth rather small, with a metal collar that is joined to a space suit of flexible and shiny fabric. We notice mysterious bracelets (…) and a mysterious device on the belly… Those who have met these extraterrestrial pilots describe them as fascinating for their intelligence, dignity and sympathy, and especially for their sincere and selfless friendship which they show and which inspires those who have met them. But what would happen if their photographs were published in our newspapers? It would result in a grotesque carnival, worthy of our stupid malignancy."
–Alberto Perego, *L' aviazione di altri pianeti opera tra noi: rapporto agli italiani: 1943-1963*, pp.532-534.

along similar lines: "... the form pattern seems to be universal. And that is not only in the human form, but we speak of all forms, except that as we view these planets finding each one ahead of the other in advancement, so each is ahead of the other in the quality of form structure, which seems to have a tendency towards perfection."[12]

With Adamski, several other contactees such as Wilbert Smith, Bruno Ghibaudi, Howard Menger, and Buck Nelson maintained that their space contacts originated from planets within our own solar system, even though some of them buckled under the pressure of public ridicule and retracted their accounts in later years. Yet our probes have so far failed to detect even monocellular life forms around our Sun. So with the Italian-American physicist – and, by the way, creator of the world's first nuclear reactor – Enrico Fermi, we may ask: If probability tells us there should be millions of civilizations in the Universe, why haven't we found any of them? Maybe there is an explanation that is as simple as it is involved.

A few months before *Flying Saucers Have Landed* was published, George Adamski wrote to a correspondent about a follow-up book he planned to write that "will clear this present state of confusion" and "even bring out a new and clearer phase of occult [= hidden] understanding which will blend perfectly with our present science ..."[13] Although the intended volume did not materialise, the following synthesis of findings from various disciplines may help to shed light on this mystery. Here is how I summarized it elsewhere:[14]

Based on its calculations of the mass of the Universe astrophysics says it doesn't know what more than 90 per cent of the cosmos consists of and hypothesizes 'dark matter' and 'dark energy' to explain this 'missing' mass. It was the Swiss astronomer Fritz Zwicky who first proposed the concept of 'dark matter', which some scientists now see as a different kind of sub-atomic particle in a 'supersymmetrical' parallel universe "that behaves like an invisible mirror-image of ordinary matter."[15] Dr Zwicky worked at the Palomar Observatory and is said to have visited Adamski three times at the Palomar Gardens Café, although he publicly ridiculed him.[16]

In February 2022, a groundbreaking experiment at the Karlsruhe Tritium Neutrino (KATRIN) spectrometer in Germany shed further light on the mysterious stage between the visible and the invisible Universe. Reporting on the findings the Max Planck Society writes about neutrinos: "In

---

12 Adamski (1949), *Pioneers of Space*, p.223.
13 Adamski, Letter to John Williamson, June 17, 1953.
14 See Gerard Aartsen (ed.; 2022), *George Adamski – Letters to Emma Martinelli*, pp.20-21.
15 Steve Connor, 'The galaxy collisions that shed light on unseen parallel Universe'. *The Independent*, 26 March 2015. See: <www.independent.co.uk/news/science/the-galaxy-collisions-that-shed-light-on-unseen-parallel-universe-10137164.html>.
16 Don Lago, 'Messages from Space'. *Michigan Quarterly Review*, Vol.54, No.1, Winter 2015. See: <hdl.handle.net/2027/spo.act2080.0054.108>.

cosmology they play an important role in the formation of large-scale structures, while in particle physics their tiny but non-zero mass sets them apart, pointing to new physics phenomena beyond our current theories."[17]

According to Patrick Decowski, a physicist with the Dutch National Institute for Subatomic Physics (Nikhef), this means there is something special about the particle: "We suspect the neutrino to hold the key to all kinds of things that physics at present doesn't understand." He thinks it could be the source of the elusive 'dark matter'.[18] Although tentatively, science itself now seems to be on the verge of acknowledging that there is no demarcation line, or separation between the physical, visible Universe and that which it can't see.

In the nineteenth century French physicist Jacques Fresnel proposed the existence of 'aether' as the invisible element that fills all space, which a theosophical writer explained as follows:

---

17 The Max Planck Society, 'Neutrinos are lighter than 0.8 electronvolts: Experiment limits neutrino mass with unprecedented precision". Phys.org, February 14, 2022. See: <phys.org/news/2022-02-neutrinos-lighter-electronvolts-limits-neutrino.html>.

18 George van Hal, 'Wereldrecord: fysici leggen neutrino op "weegschaal" en noteren duizelingwekkend lage massa'. *De Volkskrant*, February 14, 2022. See: <www.volkskrant.nl/nieuws-achtergrond/wereldrecord-fysici-leggen-neutrino-op-weegschaal-en-noteren-duizelingwekkend-lage-massa~b309d9a9/>.

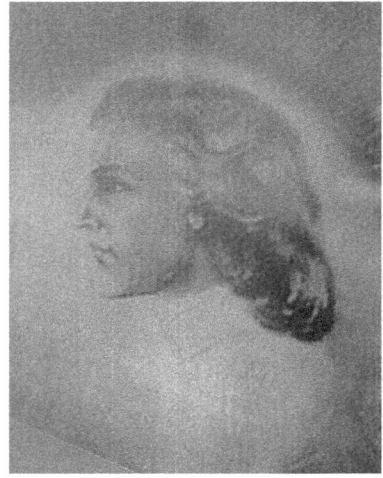

Above: Portrait of 'Orthon' painted by George Adamski.

(Images: *O Cruzeiro*/João Martins)

EXHIBIT #5: EXTRATERRESTRIAL LIFE

"That which science postulates as ether is found by occult chemistry to be not a homogeneous body, but simply another state of matter; not itself a new kind of substance, but ordinary matter reduced [i.e. rarefied; GAa] to a particular state. We may have, for example, hydrogen in an etheric condition instead of as a gas..."[19] When experiments failed to prove Fresnel's theory, science abandoned the notion of 'ether' as a universal substance.

Before quantum mechanics gave us revolutionary insights into the nature of matter, Alice A. Bailey, a teacher in the wisdom tradition wrote that the atom "can be expressed in terms of force or energy. (...) The word 'substance' itself means that which 'stands under', or which lies back of things. All, therefore, we can predicate in connection with the ether of space is that it is the medium in which energy or force functions... Substance is the ether in one of its many grades, and is that which lies back of matter itself."[20]

Systems scientist Ervin Laszlo explains that the nineteenth century idea of 'ether' has now re-entered physics as the 'deep dimension' beyond spacetime, known as the 'implicate order', the

---

19 C.W. Leadbeater (1902), *Man Visible and Invisible*, p.8.
20 Alice A. Bailey (1922), *The Consciousness of the Atom*, pp.36-37.

Page 56 left, and right: George Adamski at Palomar Terraces with the painting he had commissioned, based on his description, of his space contact whom he called Orthon. The artist was Grace May Betts (1883-1978), a painter of landscapes and Native Americans, who also did artwork for magazines and children's books, as well as the Theosophical Society and Universal Brotherhood in Point Loma, California. Between 1936 and 1946 she lived in Laguna Beach, the artists colony on the California coast were Adamski was active as a metaphysics teacher with the Royal Order of Tibet between 1933 and 1940.

'akashic field' or the 'complex plane', which "appears to be a dimension or domain of the physical world beyond spacetime".[21] [End of quote]

Adamski himself already hinted at the solution to physics' conundrum when he wrote: "All Nature is etheric; whether in a form or formless state . . . when the word 'ether' is properly understood, you can see it has no reference to spirits or disembodied entities."[22] Elsewhere he put it thus: "The trouble with the metaphysical setup is that everything in the invisible is labelled 'spiritual' while in the visible it is labelled 'material', but in truth there is neither spiritual nor material – it is all the same . . ."[23] In other words, everything – physical or spiritual – exists at some point on the continuum of the same cosmic reality, from the dimensions beyond spacetime to the three dimensions of our limited carbon-based reality. From a different angle, physicist and Noble Prize winner Erwin Schrödinger confirmed the non-existence of a boundary between the objective (physical) and subjective (spiritual) universe when he said: "Subject and object are only one. The barrier between them cannot be said to have broken down . . . for this barrier does not exist."[24]

To summarize, then, life is more abundant than previously thought, even if it exists in that 90 per cent of the Universe that astrophysics is currently unable to detect. And wherever life manifests and evolves into complex forms, this likely happens along similar lines as the life forms we know here on Earth.

The self-declared limitations of astrophysics' observations and the advancing insights into the nature of reality (see also Exhibit #6: Consciousness) strongly suggest that life manifests not only in carbon-based forms as it does on Earth, but may just as well exist in matter of a subtler nature, which conventional physics is now tentatively exploring, and for which Kirlian photography, Wilhelm Reich's 'orgone radiation', and Rupert Sheldrake's tested hypothesis of 'morphogenetic fields' may prove to be trailblazing evidence.

And thus far, this seems to be the only viable answer to Fermi's Paradox, as well as the explanation for why our probes haven't found carbon-based life on Mars or Venus, or why the appearance of extraterrestrial craft in our skies varies from lights in the sky and nebulous disc-shaped clouds to shiny metallic objects, as they lower their rate of vibration from their original etheric phase to the dense physical – passing through or remaining in any or all of the different states of matter that fall within our range of vision.

---

21 Ervin Laszlo (2016), *What is Reality? The New Map of Cosmos and Consciousness*, pp.19-20.
22 Adamski (1957), *Cosmic Science* bulletin Part 1, Question 12.
23 Aartsen (ed.; 2022), op cit, p.81.
24 Erwin Schrödinger (1958), *Mind and Matter*. As reprinted in Schrödinger, *What is Life*, combined 1967 ed., p.127.

EXHIBIT #6: CONSCIOUSNESS

While attending a lecture by crop circle investigator Colin Andrews in February 2012, UFO researcher Grant Cameron had what he calls a "download experience", which led him to realize that the answer to the UFO subject was consciousness: "It's all connected. It's all the same stuff . . . You have a field of consciousness that is everything . . ."[1] In his book *Managing Magic: The Government's UFO Disclosure Plan*, Cameron concludes: "Consciousness is the elephant in the room when it comes to full disclosure, and it is a key component to the mystery. Including the role of consciousness in the disclosure announcement will lead to the collapse of scientific materialism in (. . .) the mother of all paradigm shifts."[2]

At the beginning of the 20th century, theoretical physicist Max Planck discovered that not atoms, but minute bundles of energy (or *quanta*) make up our objective reality, which led him

to conclude: "There is no matter as such; it exists only by virtue of a force bringing the particle to vibration and holding it together . . . we must assume behind this force the existence of a conscious and intelligent mind."[3]

Planck's insights laid the foundation for what we now know as quantum physics, which has caused not only a revolution in physics, but has also called into question the scientific method based on empirical reductionism as the only reliable way of knowing anything about reality, which leaves no room for subjective experiences, including spiritual or religious realizations.

After World War 2, writes MIT professor of physics David Kaiser, physicists around the world were "torn from their pre-war routines and thrust into projects of immediate, worldly significance

---

1   Interview with Grant Cameron on *Earth Mystery News*, April 25, 2016. See: <www.youtube.com/watch?v=UaRbGSmQ4oQ>.
2   Grant Cameron (2017), *Managing Magic. The Government's UFO Disclosure Plan*, p.275.
3   Max Planck (1944), 'The Nature of Matter'.

– radar, the atomic bomb, and dozens of lesser known gadgets – physicists' day-to-day activities in 1945 bore little resemblance to those of 1925", when they were engrossed in philosophical deliberations to make sense of the quantum description of matter and energy at the atomic level.[4]

In his fascinating history of modern physics, professor Kaiser shows that what is now the cutting edge of physics only began to make its revolutionary impact in the 1970s through the "unstructured brainstorming sessions" of a hippie group of physicists who founded the Fundamental Fysiks Group in 1975 and the Physics/Consciousness Research Group in 1977. Co-founded by theoretical physicist Jack Sarfatti, the latter received cash from a "wealthy UFO enthusiast"[5] that allowed them to rent an office space in San Francisco. The lecture series they developed included topics such as "science and religion in an uncertain quantum reality", and "possibilities for communication with extraterrestrials".[6]

Returning quantum physics to more "philosophical deliberations" in the 1970s, the young physicists soon began to explore the connection between the laws of physics and the nature of consciousness. According to Kaiser the hippie physicists reshaped physics mainly by their "concerted push on Bell's theorem".[7] Physicist Joseph Bell was the first to use terms like "non-locality" and "entanglement", which suggest a scientific underpinning for the view that all life is one and interconnected. It provides a possible foundation for parapsychological phenomena such as 'remote viewing', telepathy, and other means of extra-sensory perception, or ESP. The same topics have been researched since 1973 by the Institute of Noetic Sciences (IONS), founded by Edgar Mitchell, and the Scientific and Medical Network (SMN) in the UK.

One of the first physicists to grasp the implications of the new quantum understanding of reality, Fritjof Capra, presented these in the context of Eastern mysticism in his thought-

---

4   David Kaiser (2011), *How the Hippies Saved Physics. Science, Counterculture, and the Quantum Revolution*. p.xiii.
5   Ibidem, p.105.
6   Ibid., p.107.
7   Ibid., pp.xxiv-xxv.

EXHIBIT #6: CONSCIOUSNESS

DISCLOSED: ADAMSKI – 1932

Now people are beginning to get into the consciousness of the invisible world from which all things come forth. They are acquainting themselves with the ALL instead of the parts.

(*The Invisible Ocean*, 1932)

provoking book *The Tao of Physics*. The inspiration for his book came from an experience of interconnectedness he had on the beach in Santa Cruz, where he "'saw' cascades of energy coming down from outer space, in which particles were created and destroyed in rhythmic pulses; I 'saw' the atoms of the elements and those of my body participating in this cosmic dance of energy…"[8] Other well-known examples of similar experiences include astronaut Edgar Mitchell's epiphany of the oneness of life while he was on the Apollo 14 mission returning from the Moon, and the experience that neurosurgeon Eben Alexander had while in a coma, even though he did not believe in the reality of near-death experiences before that.

In a recent report for the SMN, psychologist Harald Walach calls such experiences "radical introspection", which are "too rich to be pressed in the structure of simple sentences, and to be submitted to exclusive logic" due perhaps "to the fact that such direct, radically introspective experiences of reality touch upon the deep structure of reality from within."[9] As a further illustration, Grant Cameron described his 'download' experience and the "absolute certainty" with which he gained his insights as "instantaneous".

In his report, professor Walach challenges the prevailing scientific background assumptions that take material entities as the only 'real' elements in the Universe, and argues that we need a post-materialist science "that takes seriously phenomena, experiences and concepts that have to do with consciousness in a very broad sense."[10] This would include non-local experiences such as out-of-body experiences, near-death experiences or radical introspective experiences.

Recognizing the need for an expanded science, UFO researcher Morris K. Jessup once wrote: "The progress of Science in accumulating quantitative knowledge has been tremendous – but it has resulted in ever narrowing channels of refinement defined by an ever-increasing number of

---

8   Fritjof Capra (1975), *The Tao of Physics*, first UK edition, p.9.
9   Harald Walach (2019), *Beyond a Materialist Worldview. Towards an Expanded Science*, pp.80-81.
10 Ibidem, p.9.

decimal places. Qualitatively, the intellectuality of Science has been largely pauperized by the exclusion of 'erratics' and that vast realm of reality which Science has chosen to call 'immaterial'."[11] Echoing George Adamski's notion that in reality there is no distinction between the spiritual and the material (see page 58), Jessup says: "We must cease to think that unexplained phenomena are 'supernatural,' for we must realize that 'Nature' is composed of all things, physical and spiritual: the universe or the 'omniverse'."[12] After all, as David Kaiser says, ". . . our natural inclination to analyze systems into subsystems, and to build up knowledge of the whole from careful study of its parts, grinds to a halt in the quantum domain."[13]

Science philosopher Philip Goff summarizes the argument for post-materialist science as follows: "In recent years we have gotten used to taking 'science' and 'physical science' to be synonymous. At the same time, we look to scientists to give us a complete theory of reality. These two demands on science cannot be reconciled. So long as 'science' is equated with 'physical science,' it will be . . . unable to account for consciousness . . . [and] confined to telling us what matter does, remaining silent on its intrinsic nature."[14] We can see how Morris Jessup was rather ahead of his time with his analysis that the errors of science were "errors of omission rather than commission. For the greater part, Science is right – *as far as it goes*."[15]

The 'hippie physicists' in the 1970s set quantum physics on the path to where the 'new' generation of post-materialist scientists now posit a grand new view of the Universe as an ocean of consciousness. Since then the scientific vanguard has made massive strides, which systems philosopher Ervin Laszlo summarizes as follows: "With the advent of quantum physics, we can now say what the universe truly is with more confidence than ever before. We can now conceive of the universe as a field of vibration, of which the elements are individual vibrations that resonate together and create more complex clusters of vibration. (. . .) *The cosmos is consciousness*."[16] What is more, "The evident purpose of evolution in [the universe] is to achieve coherence in the domain of natural systems, and embracing oneness in the sphere of consciousness."[17]

Readers who object that this is all speculation because philosophy cannot take the place of hard science, would do well to remember, as Philip Goff points out, that Galileo refuted one of the central claims of Aristotle's physics – that heavy objects fall to the ground faster than light

---

11 M. K. Jessup (1956), *UFO and the Bible*, p.24.
12 Ibid., p.30.
13 Kaiser (2011), op cit, p.37.
14 Philip Goff (2019), *Galileo's Error. Foundations for a New Science of Consciousness*, p.129.
15 Jessup (1956), op cit, p.54.
16 Ervin Laszlo (2022), *The Upshift. Wiser Living on Planet Earth*, p.120, p.124.
17 Laszlo (2017), *The Intelligence of the Cosmos. New Answers from the Frontiers of Science*, p.46.

objects, "not with observation or experiment but with a philosophical thought experiment."[18] Paradoxically, the fundamental nature of consciousness is also suggested in a recent study by an astrophysicist and a neurosurgeon who documented the striking similarities between cosmic networks of galaxies and neural networks of brain cells, based on a quantitative analysis of neural and cosmic networks. Their findings, strikingly illustrated in the photos below, showed that cosmic physical processes and planetary biological processes lead to similar structures even with differences in scale greater than 27 orders of magnitude.[19]

Nevertheless, as is to be expected, many scientists who swear by the incontestability of their empirical background assumptions feel their discipline is under attack from 'pseudo' science. One well-known example is the popular cognitive psychologist Steven Pinker who calls extrasensory perception and other non-local experiences "paranormal woowoo", and asked: "Why do so many of us believe in so much quackery and flapdoodle?"[20] One wonders if Dr Pinker is aware that the

---

18 Goff (2019), op cit, p.62.
19 Franco Vazza and Alberto Feletti. 'The Quantitative Comparison Between the Neuronal Network and the Cosmic Web'. *Frontiers of Physics*, November 16, 2020 <www.frontiersin.org/articles/10.3389/fphy.2020.525731/full>.
20 'In touch with reality' on *Think with Pinker*. December 2, 2021. See: <www.bbc.co.uk/sounds/play/m001214x>.

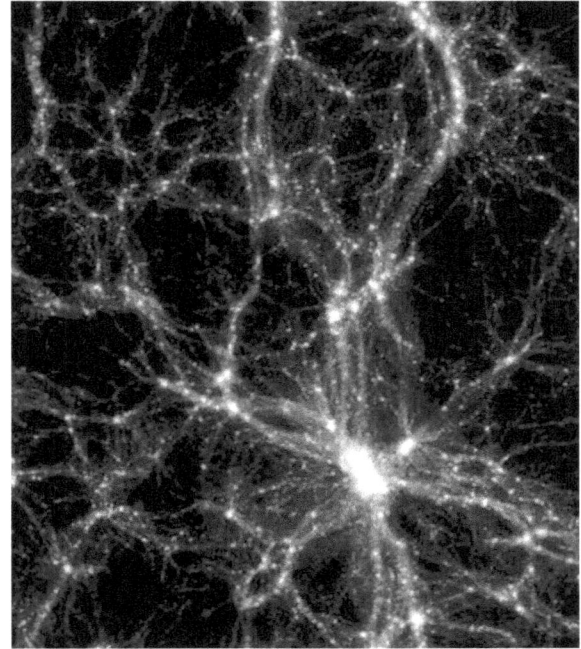

(Image: Springel & others / Virgo Consortium)

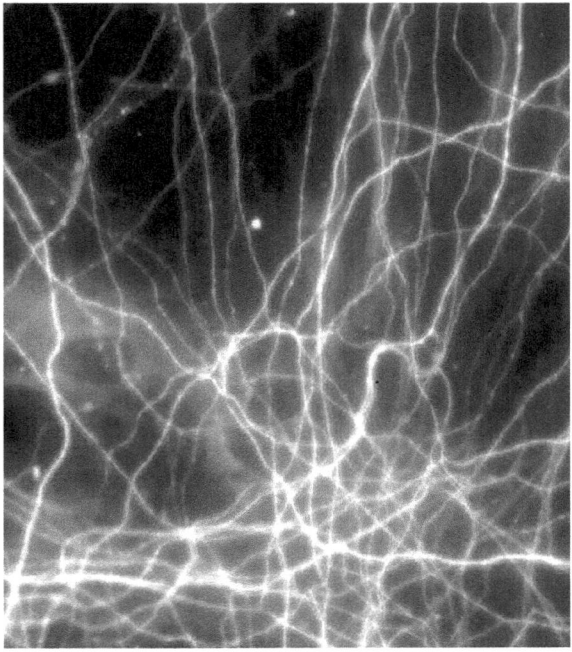

(Image: Center for Brain Injury and Repair, University of Pennsylvania School of Medicine)

Left: Computer simulation showing the cosmic web of gaseous filaments that connect galaxies in the Universe. Right: Axons (nerve fibres) in the brain are reaching out to connect with other neurons.

'father' of modern psychology, William James, was a member of the Theosophical Society, whose founder was the first in modern times to propose the primacy and evolution of consciousness.[21]

Pinker maintains that the laws of physics are completely adequate and we don't need "strange new forces or fields to explain how my bicycle works, or why eclipses happen". Ironically, when young Max Planck sought study advice from his teacher in 1874, he was already told that physics was an "almost fully developed science which ... would soon have assumed its final stable form."[22] Until 25 years later Planck laid the foundation for what would become the quantum revolution in physics . . .

In a response to Pinker's dismissal of post-materialist science, Cambridge University professor of physics and Nobel laureate Brian Josephson writes: "It happens all the time in

science that people consider, on the basis of the evidence available at the time, that they have a good understanding of some particular state of affairs. But then something new comes up that doesn't fit the existing scheme, and as a result the models have to be adjusted to take them into account. (. . .) Thus, the idea that we can have 'complete understanding' of nature in a particular domain is a misconceived one."[23]

While the latest insights into consciousness as the fundamental nature of reality are still disputed and seen as 'fringe' or 'pseudo' science by 'hardcore materialists' like Steven Pinker, let us not forget that at one point the same was true for the notion that the Earth is not the centre of the Universe, or that life is not exclusive to Earth. Such expanding notions should be seen as tangential evidence that consciousness evolves and expands, even if it doesn't do so at the same

---

21 Sylvia Cranston (1993), *HPB. The Extraordinary Life & Influence of Helena Blavatsky, Founder of the Modern Theosophical Movement*, p.xx.
22 Max Planck (1943), *Wege zur Physikalischen Erkenntnis. Reden und Vorträge*, Band 1, p.128.
23 Brian Josephson, 'Comments on Steven Pinker's view of the Paranormal'. March 22, 2022. See: <opensciences.org/comments-on-steven-pinker-s-view-of-the-paranormal>.

EXHIBIT #6: CONSCIOUSNESS

pace in every individual, scientists included. And perhaps we can take comfort from Max Planck's observation that, "A new scientific truth does not triumph by convincing its opponents and making them see the light, but rather because its opponents eventually die, and a new generation grows up that is familiar with it."[24]

The new scientific understanding of reality is fast gaining ground among academic philosophers, where a majority of only 56.5 per cent 'materialists' remains.[25] However, its intangible and therefore difficult to substantiate nature made the consciousness aspect of the UFO phenomenon anathema for much of the last 70 years among 'serious' UFO researchers, who held on to the strictly 'materialist' approach of gathering physical or visual evidence, despite the UFO proving to be as elusive as matter itself. Yet, after the US Air Force retrieved the wreckage and casualties from a crashed saucer in July 1947, Grant Cameron says, based on scrutinizing hundreds of previously classified documents, "on day one, when this thing starts, they realize there's this mental aspect, and realize what we would learn later, is that's how you fly the craft. You use your mind."[26] This was also witnessed by George Adamski, who observed that the various types of instruments on the ship on which he was invited, "were not ordinary ones since they were subject to the pilots' own consciousness."[27]

In a recent blog post Cameron compiled statements from various experts and contactees that indicate a consciousness-machine symbiosis is key to understanding the propulsion used by extraterrestrial craft.[28] Steven Greer concurs, saying: "The biggest secrets are not the zero-point energy and electrogravitics, it's the science of consciousness. It's the trans-dimensional physics that go interfacing with thought and consciousness." And: "Their [the ETs] whole paradigm is non-locality in physics, alright, where things can be in multiple places at once. (. . .) All their communications systems are moving through the consciousness field and are thought-actuated."[29]

If, as Cameron says, "consciousness is the elephant in the room when it comes to full disclosure", rather than urging the authorities to share the "secret" of the consciousness aspect of the UFO phenomenon, Dr Greer could just consult George Adamski's body of work, which reveals everything the visitors think is safe to share with people of Earth. For now. For, even

---

24 Planck, as quoted in Thomas Kuhn (1970 ed.), *The Structure of Scientific Revolutions*, p.150.
25 Goff (2019), op cit, p.121.
26 Alex Tsarakis (2016), 'UFO researcher Grant Cameron has uncovered 100s of previously classified UFO documents pointing toward a UFO/consciousness link'. *Skeptiko*, August 11, 2016. See: <skeptiko.com/grant-cameron-ufo-consciousness-link-324/>.
27 George Adamski (1962), *Special Report* (Part 2), p.1.
28 Cameron, 'Consciousness, Flying Saucers and the Intergalactic Computer Network'. Whitehouse UFO, January 30, 2022. See: <whitehouseufo.blogspot.com/2022/01/consciousness-flying-saucers-and.html>.
29 Blake Cousins, Brent Cousins (dir.; 2022), *Above Top Secret: The Technology Behind Disclosure*.

if largely unacknowledged, the notion of consciousness being fundamental was central to Adamski's accounts and teaching throughout his mission, often in strikingly similar phrases as those now used by post-materialist scientists. Read, for instance, how Adamski describes the nature of reality in his first publication, *The Invisible Ocean*. Here he likens the Universe to an ocean where the strata of pressure represent the various grades of consciousness: "... I am in the invisible ocean of vibrations or consciousness."[30] Eighty-five years later, professor Ervin Laszlo writes: "The universe, as we now know, is not a domain of matter moving in passive space and indifferently flowing time; it is a sea of coherent vibrations."[31]

Adamski elaborates: "We call the invisible ocean spirit, force, or power. In this great spirit of God we are all swimming like a lot of little fish. We realize this as we grow in consciousness."[32] And: "This invisible ocean of ours is so great that we are like grains of sand in it. It has no limits. No matter how high man goes into consciousness, it will still have no limits for him. No man can measure its power. Everything is right here."[33] Likewise, in his final body of teachings, the *Science of Life* study course: "We must remember that consciousness is the sea of life within which all forms are living, regardless of what they may be."[34]

In an article from the 1930s Adamski outlined the relation between mind, matter and consciousness: "Until quite recently mind and matter have been considered as widely separated as the poles. The materialists have exalted matter into predominance and the metaphysicians have given the supremacy to the mind while consciousness has received scarcely a consideration. (. . .) Evolution is not the expression of mind but the expansion of the mind. Mind is only the channel of expression, the avenue by which consciousness manifests itself into matter. Body, mind and consciousness are one and inseparable. Matter would cease to exist if it were not supported by consciousness. Consciousness could not express itself in matter if it were not for the mind over which it travels and mind would be useless if it were not acting as a channel between the two."[35]

In *Pioneers of Space* he explains: "In the beginning, form is preceded by what might be called an imaginary complete picture of what the form is to be... So the invisible thought or picture may be called imaginary but it is real and can be brought into material or solidified manifestation. Of course back of this life force manifestation is its perception and birth. Back of all forms lies the

---

30 Adamski (1932), *The Invisible Ocean*, pp.10-11.
31 Laszlo (2017), op cit, p.21.
32 Adamski (1932), op cit, p.6.
33 Ibid., p.10.
34 Adamski (1964), *Science of Life*, Lesson Eleven.
35 Adamski (n.d.), 'Body, mind and consciousness'. Reprinted in *UFO Contact*, Vol.3 No.6, December 1966, pp.158-59.

EXHIBIT #6: CONSCIOUSNESS

Fatherly intelligence..."[36] In May 1955, about the development of a human embryo, he rightfully remarked: "... let's honestly admit that we don't know a thing about how life is created. Yet there is something in there that knows what to do." And in answer to a question: "That which you see is quite real, but it is not the essence or pure source of reality. It is only the effects of the real. That which you see is also real, but it is a temporal real or an effect."[37] Yet, he said elsewhere, "the consciousness had to be before the building, or house within I live, could have been built."[38]

When professor Laszlo writes that the clusters of coordinated vibration, or quanta, that make up our objective world "are 'in-formed' by a factor we identify as an underlying cosmic intelligence"[39], it is remarkable to read how Adamski said virtually the same in 1964: "Consciousness is the father and mother of all form creation which conceives and gives birth to the various forms. And within it is the blueprint or memory which is ever present..."[40]

Adamski claims his journey in *Pioneers of Space* took place as an out-of-body experience by projecting his consciousness afar, which builds directly on his teaching about consciousness in *The Invisible Ocean*. It also portends how he later taught his students to acquire the same

(Images: *O Cruzeiro*/João Martins)

ability in his *Science of Life* course, just like 'remote viewing' has been researched and taught to members of various international intelligence agencies since the 1950s by, for instance, Harold Puthoff and Russell Targ at the Stanford Research Institute.[41]

It should not surprise us then how, in correspondence with a student, Adamski explains that his experiences in *Pioneers of Space* should not be understood as physical but as out-of-body experiences, saying: "Yes, one may travel at will [to] any place in the universe without taking his

---

36 Adamski (1949), *Pioneers of Space*, pp.185-86.
37 Adamski, 'Private Group lecture for Advanced Thinkers', May 4, 1955, p.11, p.12.
38 Gerard Aartsen (2022), *George Adamski – Letters to Emma Martinelli*, p.65.
39 Laszlo (2016), *What is Reality? The New Map of Cosmos and Consciousness*, p.9.
40 Adamski (1964), op cit, Lesson Seven.
41 Harold E. Puthoff, 'CIA-Initiated Remote Viewing At Stanford Research Institute'. Institute for Advanced Studies, 1996. See: <www.biomindsuperpowers.com/Pages/CIA-InitiatedRV.html> (archived).

physical body since the physical is not man, but rather the house of man."[42] Knowing full well that the world was not ready to accept this he confirms, "to others I keep silent about this."[43]

It was in his *Science of Life* course, of which the final lesson was released only months before his death, that Adamski elaborates how consciousness may operate separately from the body that serves as its vehicle in the three-dimensional world of physical objects. He describes an example of his ability to do so during his time as a metaphysics teacher in Laguna Beach. However, he says, "when my interest was taken up with flying saucers these experiences ceased"[44] – probably because they were no longer necessary when he was frequently invited on board the visitors' space craft. Also, as he explains how we may learn to direct our consciousness elsewhere, he explicitly distinguishes between his travels in consciousness and his "trips in space craft taken bodily".[45]

While more and more scientists are beginning to see matter as a mere 'shadow' of an underlying fundamental consciousness, the non-locality of consciousness postulated by the pioneers of quantum research is only now gradually being more widely accepted. But long before this became a familiar concept through quantum science and consciousness research, George Adamski explained it in layman's terms as follows: "... if we were to know ourselves as we should, there is no place to go – here or hereafter. We are already everywhere. The only thing that governs location is the interest that the individual has [i.e. where we focus our attention; GAa]. It is as the great Master said, wherever a man's heart is, that is where he is. If a man can lose location, there is only one other place he can find himself in – that is in the totality of the universe."[46]

It was in fact the revolutionary work of physicist David Bohm that predicted the non-locality of the world, i.e. the interconnectedness of the Universe. But according to a recent documentary about his life and work, "Bohm's progressive ideas were a threat to the scientific establishment at a time when they were focused on one thing alone: The Atomic Bomb."[47]

Faced with the evidence presented here, detractors as well as disclosure advocates who have spurned Adamski's accounts until now must decide how it is possible that he taught the fundamental nature and non-locality of consciousness at a time when physicists were preoccupied with developing ever more destructive weaponry, rather than exploring the connection between the laws of physics and the nature of consciousness. Was it prescience, or was it his personal ability and experience? Either way, Adamski's information stands confirmed, again.

---

42 Aartsen (2022), op cit, p.63.
43 Ibid., p.38.
44 Adamski (1964), op cit, Lesson Eleven.
45 Ibid., Lesson Five.
46 Aartsen (2022), op cit, p.37.
47 Paul Howard (dir.; 2020), *Infinite Potential: The Life & Ideas of David Bohm*.

EXHIBIT #7: PARADIGM SHIFT

"The main thing is NOT a question of saucers, my experiences or anybody else's. The main thing is WHAT IS REALLY TRANSPIRING IN THIS WORLD. THAT is more important than any individual or phenomena that is taking place at this moment."

–George Adamski[1]

If the preceding exhibits succeeded in weaning the reader off the prevailing view of George Adamski as deluded or a fraud, you may be more open to the argument in this, the final exhibit, for which, despite much circumstantial evidence in world developments, admittedly, there are no statements or materials from relevant institutions or disciplines that substantiate his pronouncements.

Arguably, one of the main things transpiring in the outer world is the rapid pace at which our global society has become one and interconnected, reflecting the waxing consensus about the nature of reality that emerges from the quantum revolution in science. Information and communication technologies allow our social media to alert us instantly of major events happening anywhere on Earth, whether it be a natural disaster, a scientific breakthrough, or something of similar import; like the break-up of a celebrity couple, or the latest immature display of obscene riches by a tech billionaire or someone else with more cents than sense.

That something is seriously afoot in our world can also be gleaned from the growing number of people and organisations that are looking for a 'new paradigm' – a new way of looking at the world and life, stemming from the old Greek *paradeigma*, or 'pattern'. As anyone who doesn't manage to avoid the news headlines will be aware, our present mode of living is causing severe crises, and our old and trusted political and economic structures no longer seem fit for purpose.

---

1 George Adamski at a press conference with ministers in Detroit, September 1955. See: Adamski (1974), *Many Mansions*, p.3.

≡ TIME   APRIL 21, 2021 7:00 AM EDT

Judith Butler: Creating an Inhabitable World for Humans Means Dismantling Rigid Forms of Individuality

The late professor of international history Arnold Toynbee reportedly stated that great civilisations are not murdered but instead, take their own lives. It is, of course, debatable whether a civilization that accepts bewildering social inequality[2], tolerates 50 million of its people to live and work in slavery[3], and hesitates to curb the destruction of its own planetary habitat – to retain the outmoded concept of economic growth on a planet with finite resources[4] – qualifies as "great". But that humanity is on a fast track to taking its own life if we don't radically alter our course was highlighted again when the United Nations published its Global Assessment Report on Disaster Reduction 2022, titled *Our World At Risk*. Although the first warning along these lines appeared as long ago as 1972 as the *Limits to Growth* report, written by the Club of Rome, *Our World At Risk* is the first time a UN report warns of "the collapse of human civilisation".[5]

Unfortunately, as people sense the inevitability of change and perceive the ensuing uncertainties of the time, they cling to politicians and world views that promise them ways to hold on to the old certainties for just a bit longer – even if it leaves their grandchildren without a habitable planetary home. Better the devil you know, seems to be the preferred coping mechanism...

If we are to know what the new paradigm for life on Earth might be, we should first understand what the current paradigm is or why it is outdated. To do this, let us imagine for a moment that we could get onto a spaceflight and, like Edgar Mitchell beholding planet Earth from space, we take a similar holistic look at how humanity has evolved over the past 2,000 years. Perhaps we would see that our current way of looking at life and the world is based on the precepts that we have internalised during that time – as we began to grow out of the herd mentality that characterized most of humankind in the ancient world.

Observing carefully, we might see that what we have learned is that we each have our own

---

2 'What is global inequality?' Oxfam, November 23, 2022. See: <https://www.oxfamamerica.org/explore/stories/what-is-global-inequality/>.
3 '50 million people worldwide in modern slavery'. ILO press release, September 12, 2022. See: <https://www.ilo.org/global/about-the-ilo/newsroom/news/WCMS_855019/lang--en/index.htm>.
4 'What is ecocide?'. See: <https://www.stopecocide.earth/what-is-ecocide>.
5 Nafeez Ahmed, 'UN Warns of 'Total Societal Collapse'. *Byline Times*, May 26, 2022. See: <https://bylinetimes.com/2022/05/26/un-warns-of-total-societal-collapse-due-to-breaching-of-planetary-boundaries/>.

EXHIBIT #7: PARADIGM SHIFT

> "If man is to live without catastrophe, he must look upon his fellow being as himself, the one a reflection of the other."
>
> *(Inside the Space Ships*, 1955)

individuality, which is unique and invaluable, that we have our own individual responsibility, and we should not let others be our authority. Readers who take the Gospels of the New Testament as vignettes to live by may recognize this lesson in the stories where Jesus of Nazareth challenged the authority of the religious leaders of his time, and urged people to think for themselves. His willingness, and that of his disciples and many who followed them, to die for their beliefs sowed the seeds for the other main characteristic that humanity has developed over the past era: idealism.

In recent history, the quality of idealism reached a preliminary climax in the global battle between 'capitalism' and 'communism'; the one claiming to champion freedom, the other justice – with neither delivering because the two cannot exist in isolation. Although fundamentalist capitalists claim their ideal has won, seen from our 'cosmic' vantage point, it is clear that with the collapse of the communist ideal both have been replaced by the neoliberal ideal of 'individualism'. Promoted as the idea of the primacy of freedom for every individual, it has actually been stripping away many basic worker and civil rights, won over the past 150 years, enabling the powerful few to exploit the many – and the planet – for their blind greed and self-indulgence.

As a result, many now interpret individual responsibility as a license to take for themselves whatever they can. Likewise, idealism has become so extreme as to be willing to let others die for your beliefs in terrorist acts of religious, political or economic fundamentalism.[6] Hence, we see today how the two qualities of individuality and idealism that humanity has acquired in its evolution over the past 2,000 years, have crystallized into their extremes. Gross selfishness, competition, intolerance, and fanaticism in the face of widespread human suffering make it clear that the old paradigm has run its course.

George Adamski might well be referring to the crystallized human qualities of the past era when he says: "For many things that God gives to us become curses when He is ready to give us something better to replace the old – not through any fault of His but through the fault of man's habitual possessiveness. You cannot have the pie and eat it too, as the old saying goes."[7]

---

6   While most readers will be familiar with the acts of religiously motivated terror perpetrated in recent times, often committed in retaliation against acts of political or military terror perpetrated by governments, for acts of economic terror see e.g. *Confessions of an Economic Hitman* by John Perkins (2004), or *The Shock Doctrine* by Naomi Klein (2007).
7   Gerard Aartsen (ed.; 2022), *George Adamski – Letters to Emma Martinelli*, pp.68-69.

> **Khaleej Times**
>
> by **Allan Jacob** Published: Tue 9 Aug 2022, 10:37 PM   00:43:33 Maghrib 17:32
>
> ## Who profits from the war economy?
>
> The Military-Industrial Complex is in the thick of the action as multiple conflicts break out and regional instability grows

Six years before President Dwight Eisenhower warned against the establishment of a 'military-industrial complex' in his farewell speech, George Adamski already hinted at such, indicating how the powers-that-be have everything to lose when that crystallization finally comes undone: "Is it because they fear the event which might bring peace and understanding among men on Earth, whereas war has become a financial investment that pays well to certain investors? (...) This knowledge of interplanetary visitors who are friendly to Earth people, and who themselves have learned to live in peace with one another seems to have given new hope to many who had lost hope; and a new purpose to Life to untold numbers. Is this what those who control the purse strings of the world fear? Acceptance of the reality of Interplanetary Visitors could and would have far-reaching effects upon the present-day economic system on Earth. Everybody would be affected in some ways, but the few would be affected in a far greater degree. I believe they see this and are fighting it with everything they have... And youthful minds filled with challenging thoughts of space travel are not so easily diverted toward the rather questionable honor awaiting in bloody battlefields. Is this what the financiers see and fear? I think it is!"[8]

In his article 'The Scientist and the UFO', Frank B. Salisbury, the plant physiologist who worked for NASA and also had an interest in UFOs, pondered: "It is interesting to consider the possibility that the contactees are genuine..." but, he wonders, "Why should visitors from another world bother with such obscure representatives of the human race, anyway? Their message is always that man must cease his wars or be destroyed, but why should such an important message be given to someone who is bound to be considered a liar when he delivers it?"[9]

Here we must correct Dr Salisbury. When the 1950s contactees first went public with the extraterrestrial message of the need for international cooperation toward world peace and socioeconomic justice, they met with rapidly growing interest from a public that was feeling the threat of nuclear annihilation weighing heavily on them. For instance, when George Adamski was invited to speak in Detroit, Michigan, 28 March 1954, the Detroit Masonic Hall was packed

---

8   Adamski, Letter to Gray Barker, March 11, 1955. Reproduced in Barker (1980), *The Adamski Documents*, Part 1.
9   Frank B. Salisbury, 'The Scientist and the UFO'. *BioScience* Vol.17, No.1, January 1967.

EXHIBIT #7: PARADIGM SHIFT

Why we need a new economic model centred on human rights

Guest content
09 November 2020

with 4,700 people (see page 45). While it is true that governments and the military-industrial complex, operating through the Pentagon, had been trivializing and covering up sightings and the retrieval of crashed saucers since 1947, it was the growing public interest in the contactees' message that triggered an all-out disinformation campaign aimed at confusing and scaring the war-weary populace, which even involved staging 'alien abductions' and 'cattle mutilations'. Until then, Adamski and his fellow contactees' accounts had the open-minded, if often sceptical ear of many, even in the fields of science, politics and the military.

As for why the visitors would relay "such an important message" of warning against further global conflict through "such obscure representatives", the reason may be found in the significance of this time in human history. Mass communication is constantly misused to infringe people's free will through political and commercial propaganda. Imagine if the message had been given through the Pope, the President, or – at the time – the Queen of England? It would have instantly been accepted by millions who have not yet outgrown the herd mentality. They would not necessarily respond to the inherent wisdom and logic of cooperating for the survival of the human race and the safe progress of its civilization, instead of endangering the planet's future by risking nuclear warfare, but simply bend to the authority of the esteemed messengers. Hence, the acceptance of such a call for peace would not come from an expanded perception of our place in the global community of nations and as members of the one human family, and thus lack the fundamental change of heart needed to sustain the necessary changes long-term.

The initial worldwide interest in the message that the contactees were asked to share with the world grew from people's heartfelt response to the insignificant seeds sown by "obscure" individuals sharing their accounts – and not because they had any kind of status or social standing. In the event, their number was insufficient to withstand the counter offensive from the vested interests of the military-industrial complex. And as a result we are now faced with 'disclosure' efforts by the same vested interests, which seem intended to instil the notion that confirmed unidentified aerial phenomena are posing a threat to national security.

Given the present state of the world, it is no wonder that a growing number of people are ready for new ways of looking at life and the world, new ways to organise society. This is reflected in the number of organisations that have been set up in search of such a new paradigm, perhaps not surprisingly also among UFO researchers and disclosure advocates. So in addition to, for instance, Ervin Laszlo's Institute for New Paradigm Research, we also have Steve Bassett's Paradigm Research Group and Daniel Sheehan's New Paradigm Institute, as well as a host of lesser known UFO researchers looking for a new 'pattern' of life, a new world view that the reality of the ET presence calls for. The fact that a 'new paradigm' has become something of a philosopher's stone in the fields of consciousness studies and UFO research, as I said elsewhere, indicates that the human mind is ready at a sufficient scale for a new level of understanding.

As we saw in Exhibit #6, science has found that at the most fundamental level, life and the universe are intricately connected – no-one is separate from anyone or anything on Earth or in the Universe. In Exhibit #5, about extraterrestrial life, we saw that evolution is not random but where it occurs, most likely proceeds along very similar lines. Since the worldwide availability of the Internet we take interconnectedness for granted in the area of technological connections and information exchange, but the same attitude is still sadly lacking when it comes to the social or moral implications of the fact that human life is one, and an integral part of the planet. Yet, as systems science tells us, the purpose of evolution is "to achieve coherence in the domain of natural systems, and embracing oneness in the sphere of consciousness."[10] And if evolved forms of consciousness, in the words of Ervin Laszlo, display a "mind-set that emerges in ethical, insightful, and spiritual human beings"[11], we can see where humanity is dangerously lagging behind.

To clarify, I understand professor Laszlo's use of the word 'spiritual' here as referring to not simply prayer, meditation or similar ways of seeking inner peace, but rather to any or all forms of transcending our present condition, be it physical, emotional, mental, social, et cetera. In a word, 'spiritual' may be understood as any activity that contributes to our growing awareness of Life as one and indivisible, and manifesting this in action in our daily life. In practical terms, this implies that we are 'our brother's keeper'. And while this may not be a new notion, its practical implementation according to the Golden Rule, and as stipulated in Article 25 of the UN Declaration of Human Rights, would be revolutionary in its effects of creating the trust between nations that is required for cooperating towards justice and freedom for all.

In his lectures Adamski indicated that he was well aware of the paradigm shift that is taking place, even if he described it in Christian terminology: "... it states in our own Bible that in the latter days (as we might call it at the moment) that when these things will be happening ... like 'signs in the sky and war and rumors of war' ... we will have come to an end of a cycle, or as

---

10 Ervin Laszlo (2017), *The Intelligence of the Cosmos. New Answers from the Frontiers of Science*, p.46.
11 Ibidem, p.39.

some people call it, a 'dispensation.'"¹² He also noted the crystallization of the old paradigm that is holding us back, when he wrote to a correspondent: "Instead of recognizing the Divine plan working, man resists the change as it is being forced upon him [by cosmic circumstance; GAa] and he blames this one and that one and someone else for the wrongs which he thinks they are doing – according to his judgment of right, promoted by habits of 2,000 years."¹³

"You can see the disorder in the world which was prophesied in the Great Book. It says that at the end of the cycle the whole world will be in a disorderly state and all must decay so that a new order may enter. In other words, a cleaning of the house must take place before the new furniture can be placed in it. This is happening now."¹⁴ Although he believed the transition would take 30 years, from 1940, world conditions show us that humanity has not been ready to clean its house.

While many contactees in the 1950s concurred with Adamski's expectation of a new dispensation dawning in some form or other, he knew as no other that this is not necessarily to do with a new religion, but with the manifestation of a new phase in the evolution of consciousness – the inevitable consequence of Earth entering a new cosmic cycle that some would refer to as the transition from the age of Pisces to the age of Aquarius. And although the latter is not yet recognized or acknowledged by traditional scientists beyond the precession of the equinox¹⁵, there is now a growing understanding that consciousness, from the most limited in atoms to the most unfathomable in galaxies, is ever evolving towards greater unity. A number of advanced thinkers, such as professor Laszlo, agree that humanity stands on the threshold of a new awareness. Adamski himself put it thus: "... the world is going through a revolutionary state in which there are many characters. This drama of a revolutionary state is necessary if man is to know the world he has always dreamt about."¹⁶

Even a cursory glance today will confirm how accurate was Adamski's assessment of the volatile state of the world, as we see the structures of our old 'civilization' – political, economic, financial – failing as a result of our divisions, while environmental degradation, poverty and hunger, pollution and climate change are global problems that can only be tackled through international cooperation. As Adamski said: "For it takes thought ... UNITED THOUGHT ... to perpetuate anything ... whether it's a conflict state or a harmonious state."¹⁷

---

12 Adamski (1956), 'World of Tomorrow'. Transcript of lecture at the Detroit Institute of Arts, September 20, 1955, p.1.
13 Aartsen (ed.; 2022), op cit, p.68.
14 Adamski, 'Private group lecture for advanced thinkers'. Transcript of lecture in Detroit, May 4, 1955, p.15.
15 See e.g. David P. Stern (2007), 'Astronomy of the Earth's Motion in Space – 7. Precession'. In: *From Stargazers to Starships*. See: <pwg.gsfc.nasa.gov/stargaze/Sprecess.htm>.
16 Aartsen (ed.; 2022), op cit, p.67.
17 Adamski (1974), *Many Mansions*, p.6.

Let us return to our discussion of paradigms – old and new. If the 'old' and waning, but still prevailing paradigm is based on the qualities of individuality and idealism which humanity has acquired over the past, say, 2,000 years, what qualities can we expect from a new paradigm – or in religious terms, the new dispensation?

In order for the human kingdom, not only to survive, but to evolve beyond our current point of attainment, the way forward lies in building on the qualities we have acquired, while discarding the crystallized characteristics that are holding us back, or even threatening our existence. For humanity to survive the present crises, we should not give up our individuality or strive for uniformity, but acknowledge each individual's talents and abilities, and take responsibility to contribute these to the greater good of securing our common future and progress.

Neither should we give up idealism, but rather than being willing to die or kill for our ideals, seek common ground and cooperate to strive for the highest we can achieve as a planetary race. In other words, compete not with each other, but with our past achievements, while respecting the planet's natural limits. As Adamski said: "The spirit of competition could easily be replaced by an individual's desire to do the best he can according to his ability."[18] About life on Venus he learned: "All have their services to render, for which they have their needs fulfilled, including beauty in their possessions, but not the wasteful luxury enjoyed by a comparatively few on our planet."[19]

The keynotes for the new paradigm, therefore, are unity and synthesis, that need to be expressed in human brother- and sisterhood, international cooperation and sharing of the world's resources – as we work towards unity of the human family while celebrating and utilising our diversity. George Adamski already recognised the trend underlying the present turmoil: "There is something transpiring in this world that we never dreamed would take place in our time, but it is taking place . . . the tendency toward a United World. Why not? If we do admit there is a great power which has put us here and also created this world? I believe, myself, that this power meant for all that were placed upon this planet to be as a family, not as strangers, and go where they wish to go upon this great ball of dirt."[20]

Even before his personal extraterrestrial contacts had begun, Adamski understood: "The present civilization is beginning to realize the possibilities of a better life than they now have, and are striving to bring these possibilities into fulfilment, yet the people are going about it in the wrong way. There is no segment of society upon the Earth planet at present who lives according to the primal purpose of its Creator by which all inhabitants of other planets have

---

18 Adamski (1965), *Answers to Questions Most Frequently Asked About Our Space Visitors And Other Planets*, p.17.
19 Adamski, Letter to co-workers, March 31, 1961.
20 Adamski (1956), op cit, pp.5-6.

learned to live, thereby advancing towards greater perfection."[21]

Before readers decide our discussion in the final paragraphs is veering off too much in a metaphysical direction, let us first re-establish the fact that the latest findings in science are not at odds with the universal metaphysical (or spiritual, or religious) notions. For instance, citing many references to assumed UFO phenomena in both the Bible and the Apocrypha in his book *UFO and the Bible*, astronomer and ufologist Morris K. Jessup expressed his conviction that if only we take these Bible passages literally, the UFO phenomenon will be found to be the missing link that will help bridge the schism between science and religion. In his view, the Church, or organised religion, ignores the clear references to life as a universal occurrence in its own origin story, while Science is, in its own way, dogmatic in its "misunderstanding . . . of space, and its senseless marriage to the idea that there is no life or intelligence in space . . ."[22]

Earlier I quoted Dr Wernher von Braun lamenting the seemingly unbridgeable divide between science and religion, which he regarded as two of several possible "windows on the world" or reality (see page 9). And while I'm certain that several of the books that make up the Bible include references to events that involved visitors from space, there is something far more fundamental in every world religion that should help the more scientifically minded to recognise not only the merits of their different approaches to reality, but also the common ground that they share. This is revealed when we look at the elementary precepts that can be found in all the major world religions after stripping away centuries of dogma that was added to their original teaching later in order to 'organize' what should be 'organic'.

Extracting the essence from the particulars of the various world religions, we find they all share the same three tenets: (1) the cyclical coming or return of a Teacher (Messiah, Second Coming, fifth Buddha, tenth incarnation of Vishnu, twelfth Mahdi), (2) who brings a new revelation about the source (in religious terms: a personal God) and evolution of consciousness

---

21 Adamski (1949), *Pioneers of Space*, pp.87-88.
22 M.K. Jessup (1956), *UFO and the Bible*, p.50, p.55.

(reunion with God), which (3) needs to be given expression in the establishment of right human relations as reflected in the Golden Rule, to treat others as we ourselves want to be treated.[23]

When we compare this with how systems philosopher Ervin Laszlo synthesises his findings we will find that not UFOs, but *consciousness* provides the bridge between the scientific and the religious approach to reality, even if they arrive there from seemingly opposite directions: "The closer the clusters [of coordinated vibration; i.e. physical forms] vibrate to the deep dimension [of the cosmos], the more they are in-formed by the intelligence intrinsic to the cosmos."[24] By now we are not surprised that in his earliest teaching George Adamski said something very similar: "... we are merely improving on our instruments, our bodies, making them more and more sensitive, so that, in time, through constant improvement, we can contact Divine Mind..."[25] In other words, both science and religion can be seen as a technique to understand – or reconnect with (as in the original Latin, *re-ligare*) – the source of life and consciousness. As Arnold Toynbee pointedly stated: "Theology, not religion, is the antithesis to science."[26]

On one of his meetings with his space contacts in 1954, Adamski was informed how many different ways of worship arose as humanity became more and more divided: "But even then we continued to send others out in the hope of aiding our brothers on Earth. These men were those known as 'messiahs', and their mission was to help their Earthly brothers to return to their original understanding."[27] And in his talks he would often refer to the various ways that different religions express the same notion, replying to a question from a minister: "I have studied comparative religions, I've studied them all... I don't deny any of them. (...) Fundamentally they all speak the same language, represent the same thing... You couldn't speak to me, I couldn't speak to you if the breath was not granted to us by the same Supreme Being, whatever you may name Him."[28]

George Adamski's philosophy was often dismissed as a home-spun variety of neo-theosophical teachings. In acknowledgement of one the keynotes for the new paradigm outlined above, Adamski clarified: "Someone asked me if I was a Theosophist, or a Rosicrucian, or some kind of occultist. I'm really nothing, to tell the truth! I have never belonged to any organization in my life, never took one lesson of any kind of occult organization – never!" With the massive worldwide interest in his books, he could have easily started his own organisation but, he said: "I

23　Aartsen, 'A global crisis in consciousness ... and the age-old Laws to guide us'. *The Edge* magazine, 1 October 2018. See: <www.edgemagazine. net/2018/10/a-global-crisis-in-consciousness/>.
24　Laszlo (2016), *What is Reality? The New Map of Cosmos and Consciousness*, p.15.
25　Adamski (1932), *The Invisible Ocean*, p.15.
26　A.M. Kelley (1969), *Toynbee's Industrial Revolution, Notes and Jottings*, p.243.
27　Adamski (1955), *Inside the Space Ships*, p.182.
28　Adamski (1956), op cit, p.16.

don't believe in organizations. I believe in *cooperation*."[29]

That Adamski's philosophy was likened to Theosophy is no coincidence, because the first to propose the evolution of consciousness in modern times was Helena P. Blavatsky, co-founder of the Theosophical Society. Just as almost every other proponent of revolutionary insights, she was slandered and dismissed as a fraud. But not only was the report that denounced Madame Blavatsky in 1885 fully retracted in 1986[30], the latest scientific insights also confirm her tenets about matter, consciousness and evolution. Since, as science now concurs, consciousness evolves towards ever greater unity with the Source of life, the theosophical teachings hold that out of the human kingdom has evolved a 'spiritual' kingdom, consisting of those members of the human race who have transcended the strictly human state of consciousness, and who are known as the Masters of Wisdom. It is their 'ageless wisdom' of which George Adamski presented a succinct overview in his second publication, *Wisdom of the Masters of the Far East*. And it is from their midst, according to the teachings, that in every age or cosmic cycle, the Teachers of humanity originate.

The fact that the wisdom shared by his contacts from space in *Inside the Space Ships* reflects the teachings of the ageless wisdom merely vouches for the universality of these precepts. Adamski's contacts also indicated that, as the latest science also tells us, unless we find ways and means to embrace the new paradigm of the oneness and interconnectedness of life in the way we organise society on planet Earth, we will compete ourselves into oblivion. Or, in his words: "... either the Kingdom of Heaven will be established on this Earth – or complete annihilation of Earth's inhabitants will be the inevitable result." And although he says the initial responsibility rests on the shoulders of the religious leaders, "The choice lies with Man himself."[31]

"The time has arrived that the study of what the Brothers have already given is more important than the saucers, if we are to have a better world, or prepare ourselves for the things yet to come..." And, indicating that self-inquiry, understanding our truest interconnected nature, and our individual responsibility will provide the key to such a peaceful and sustainable future: "The individual life is more important to understand than all the spacecraft in the cosmos."[32] His hosts from space, too, echoed the ancient maxim of the Oracle of Delphi, saying that knowledge of ourselves "is the first requisite".[33]

All world religions agree that a new 'dispensation' is inaugurated by a Teacher who

---

29 Adamski, 'Private group lecture...', op cit, p.1.
30 Society for Psychical Research Press Release, May 8, 1986.
31 Adamski, 'A Challenge to Spiritual Leaders', January 1962, p.3.
32 Adamski, Letter to William T. Sherwood, April 1964. As quoted in Sherwood, 'UFO Understanding: An American Perspective', July 17, 1983.
33 Adamski (1955), op cit, pp.201-02.

reintroduces the technique to reconnect our individual consciousness with the Source of consciousness. They do so in terms befitting the expanded collective consciousness and world conditions at the time, and outline the way forward from the point of crisis that arises from the cyclic cosmic realignments – before dogmatic interpretations are superimposed when the dissemination of the teaching becomes organised religion.

Interestingly, on the notion of the decaying current order and the return of a Teacher Adamski once asked: "What chance would Jesus have if He were to return to Earth in fulfillment of Bible Prophecy? (...) Unless one's conscious perception is awakened, rather than sleeping under the blanket of materialism, how could one hope to recognize a man who in appearance would be no different from others? Were Jesus to return and be accepted, it would mean that all of our present systems would be overthrown to make way for His Cosmic Teachings. Are we prepared for this?"[34]

No, George Adamski never proclaimed the Second Coming of Jesus Christ. Neither, as it happens, have science or the Pentagon. But his pronouncement that the world is entering a new dispensation long before disclosure advocates began to explore the new paradigm that must follow the expansion of human consciousness as a result of the extraterrestrial presence, is yet more evidence of Adamski's visionary understanding.

In his 'Challenge to Spiritual Leaders', Adamski outlines the situation humanity finds itself in at this time of transition between two cosmic cycles: "We are at the final crossroads. One of two things can happen. With the aid of these Visitors we can go on to become the greatest and the *only enduring* civilization this world has ever known – enduring because the peoples of the world will be united – or we can completely annihilate one another through atomic conflict..."[35]

In original Greek, the word 'paradigm' also means 'to solemnly pronounce'. Should we live to see a Teacher emerge, we would probably recognise him by his solemn pronouncement of the value of each individual and the oneness of the human family, and that both are inextricably connected, just as are the concepts of freedom and justice for the practical expression of the new paradigm of synthesis and unity.

Either way, the new paradigm requires that every one of us take their individual responsibility to accept or reject such a declaration. If we accept it, we must embrace our human brothers and sisters as ourselves if we are to set foot on the pathway to the stars, to our cosmic origins, that extraterrestrial visitors have tried to reveal to us through the 1950s contactees – George Adamski first and foremost. True disclosure begins by acknowledging that everything about the extraterrestrial presence that has thus far been confirmed, was already revealed by his pioneering work.

---

34 Adamski (1958), *Cosmic Science*, Part 5, Question 94.
35 Adamski (1962), op cit, p.3.

BONUS MATERIAL

THE ADAMSKI BOOK OF UFO/UAP DISCLOSURE

Compiled by professor Sisir Kumar Maitra of Banaras Hindu University, Varanasi, India, *We Are Not Alone in the Universe* is a rare early Indian publication from the flying saucer era of the 1950s.

Published as a free brochure in 1958, few if any copies remain in existence. It is included here to underscore how George Adamski's account reverberated around the globe before he was maliciously discredited and ridiculed by the media, mainstream science, and especially many self-described UFO researchers in the decades after this pioneer of the original 1950s contactees passed away.

The facsimile reprint in this volume was reproduced from the copy in the archives of former Adamski associate in Switzerland Lou Zinsstag, which she donated to the University Library of Basel, Switzerland after her death in 1984.

Professor Sisir K. Maitra (1887-1963) was head of the Department of Philosophy and Dean of the Faculty of Arts at Banaras Hindu University, India, and George Adamski's main contact for the Indian chapter of the Get Acquainted Program (GAP). While on his world lecture tour Adamski was welcomed by professor Maitra during a brief stopover in Calcutta on April 17, 1959. In *Flying Saucers Farewell* he describes his arrival at Calcutta airport: "Pictures were taken as I walked down the steps from the plane, and as I reached the ground a wreath of flowers was placed around my neck."
(Image: *Sunday Standard/Indian Express*)

We are not alone in the universe

Six Essays on Flying Saucers and the significance of their appearance

By

George Adamski

Brinsley le Poer Trench

J. S. Yajnik

S. K. Maitra

S. S. Banerjee

J. Escobar Faria

For Free Distribution Only
1958.

Preface

The six essays contained in this brochure were published in a serial form in the "Sunday Standard", the Sunday edition of the "Indian Express." They deal with what is unquestionably the greatest event of the present century, namely, the appearance of space craft from other worlds. Yet unfortunately, this great event, which one of the writers of these essays has called the dawn of the New Age, has received very little publicity, not only in our country, but practically throughout the globe. If this brochure succeeds in creating interest in the public mind in this, the most momentous event of the present age and perhaps in all human history, it will have amply justified its publication.

    I cannot conclude without expressing my deep sense of gratitude to the Chairman, Express Newspapers (Private) Ltd. and the Resident Editor, "Indian Express" for their kindness in publishing these essays in a serial form in the "Sunday Standard", the Sunday edition of the "Indian Express".

S. K. Maitra

WE ARE NOT ALONE IN THE UNIVERSE

George Adamski, Palomar Terraces,
Star Route, Valley Center, California, U. S. A.

For the past twelve years the peoples of Earth have been alerted to strange craft moving soundlessly overhead. Sometimes these ships have stopped to hover, hanging motionless in the sky; sometimes they have performed fantastic manoeuvres before darting away at unbelievable speeds. They have been sighted by reputable pilots, by laymen, by the military; and have been tracked on radar screens around the world. No corner of our planet has been neglected by these space travellers as they quietly observe us and the conditions existing in our world. Yet, in spite of the fact that innumerable photographs have been taken of these craft, and that official files contain many authenticated reports, to this day no government on Earth has acknowledged their reality.

But I assure you that there are thousands of spacecraft from other worlds moving through our atmosphere. I have seen these ships. I have been inside them. I have ridden into outer space in them, far beyond the fringe of our atmosphere.

Why have you not seen them? Probably because you have not cultivated the habit of raising your eyes to the heavens. On the rare occasions when you do look skyward, do you consciously search for these silently moving ships ?, or do you merely stare blankly into the beauty of the heavens ?

These ships vary in size and shape. Some are immense by our standards, others are quite small. On occasions they will approach close to Earth, sometimes landing; but their usual procedure is to stay far out in our atmosphere, beyond the threat of our attack planes. Because we on Earth live under a smothering blanket of fear, in many nations the appearance of an unidentified object sends jet planes soaring into the sky ; so the visitors seldom come close any more.

Several years ago when world tensions were not so great, it was not so difficult for the ships from other worlds to land in remote places on our planet. Thus, it was, after several reports had come to me of landings in the deserts, that on November 20, 1952, in company with six friends, I drove to one of the southern California deserts in the hope of getting a good close-up photograph of one of these strange craft. But even in my most fervent yearnings, I had never dared anticipate an actual meeting with those who operate such ships. Therefore, you can imagine my humble gratitude, yet extreme elation when I first touched hands with a human being from another planet.*

In the six year interim I have met many space travellers, have had the honour of visiting inside their ships, and of being taken for rides into outer space. During these trips I have met men and women from Venus, Mars, Jupiter, Saturn, Uranus and Neptune. They have all told me the same story, that their home-worlds are very much like our own, with natural conditions similar to those found on earth. Proof of the validity of this is the ease with which these people acclimate to our atmosphere. They say that, contrary to the belief of our scientists, while there are some differences in atmospheric conditions on other planets

---

* Footnote : This experience is told in detail in the book **Flying Saucers Have Landed**, co-authored with Desmond Leslie.   T. Werner Laurie, London, England, publishers.

(mostly due to pressure, depending upon the planet's size) these are little more than we experience between sea level and on a mountain several thousand feet high.

Our scientists have not yet visited other planets, not even our little moon. So their statement that it is not possible for people to live on our neighbouring planets is nothing more than theory, and we know that the most profound theory of today is disproved by the fact of of to-morrow. An excellent example of this is the theory once held regarding space. At one time Earth's savants pronounced space to be a vast vacuum, with distances between planets so great that, should man ever attempt interplanetary travel, it would take generations to complete the journey.

We have long since discarded that theory, and today we are planning ships for outer space travel, as our tiny man-made satellites, reaching ever further out into space, are contributing new information that I had already published.

Even through the ages, darting back as far into antiquity as men can trace, are found accounts of these people visiting Earth. From our deepest jungles to our loftiest mountain peaks, tribal histories tell of the great ones coming from the skies to render aid and give counsel to their earthbound brothers.

All great philosophies teach of the One Universal Creator ; and admonish man to look to the Cosmos for understanding. Man, it is said, was made in the image and likeness of the Creator. If, then, there is but one Creator, and man is formed in His image, why should not mankind throughout the Cosmos be the same ? Why should we believe we stand alone ?

We know that our Earth was formed as are all planets, from the elements of space. Some, I have been told, are just reaching the place where they can support human life, while others have passed that state and are slowly disintegrating back into space. For from out of space they were born, and into space they must return. Since in Nature there is constant activity, yet by a balance undreamt-of by man, the growing planets and systems exactly balance those disintegrating. But amongst these are endless numbers of worlds supporting human life ; some far below us in development, and yet others so far beyond our present understanding that we cannot conceive their way of life.

The people on our neighbouring planets are more advanced than we on Earth. We, alone, in our system are still unable to travel outer space. Our neighbours, I have been told, have long since learnt to solve their problems without resorting to the barbaric practice of war. They have learnt to respect one another as children of the Infinite, and have overcome personal greed by working together and sharing the products of their world so that no one is in want.

Why have these ships not landed in your country ? They have. Sometime ago I received a published report of a space ship landing somewhere in India ; but the people were frightened and ran into their houses, barring the doors and covering their windows tightly. So, after lingering a while, the space ship slowly departed without its occupants having the opportunity to speak to a single person. I know it is natural for people to fear the landing of such a strange craft, but I can assure you, the space visitors need not be feared. They will help us in any way they can, but they will never force themselves upon us. In the presence of fear they quietly withdraw, for they are very alert to our feelings and recognize this emotion in us.

I am not the only man who has met the space travellers, or who has been inside their ships. There have been many throughout the world. Most have remained silent because of the scepticism and ridicule that would be heaped upon them. But the time is approaching when the people of Earth will awaken to reality, when such experiences can be discussed openly and freely; and those who are coming as friends will be so accepted. For it is with the extended hand of friendship that they visit us.

There are thousands of these visitors living on Earth, in every country, but they rarely reveal their identity. However, I can tell you this; although we are not aware of it, it has been through their tireless efforts that a flaming war has been averted...a war that easily could have destroyed our present civilization. Let us humbly pray in our hearts that their wise counsel will continue to guide the destiny of our world through these troubled times.

My second book, **Inside the Space Ships,** gives detailed accounts of my visits to the space ships. During these meetings much information was given to me about their way of life, especially regarding life on Venus. This I have passed on to the peoples of Earth in the hope that these seeds may fall on fertile soil.

WE ARE NOT ALONE

The Hon'ble Brinsley le Poer Trench
Editor, "Flying Saucer Review"

The space craft that are now being seen in our skies have been recorded throughout history, but it was not until June 24, 1947, that they first became front page news in the United States, and subsequently, in the rest of the world.

On that day, Kenneth Arnold, an American businessman, was flying his own plane near Mount Rainier, in the State of Washington, when he spotted nine huge, gleaming objects speeding along at an estimated 1,200 miles an hour. He described these objects afterwards to press reporters as being saucer-shaped. That was how the term "flying saucer" arose, and thereafter the subject became an international music hall joke.

Pilots and other trained observers who reported seeing unidentified flying objects (UFOs) in those early years were often subjected to considerable ridicule. Today, the subject is becoming a little more respectable, and pilots who report UFOs are taken in much more serious vein. It could be that the term "flying saucer" which many regarded as peculiarly unfortunate, was a good one from the standpoint of introducing the most tremendous happening of all time in a gradual light manner.

Since Arnold's sighting in 1947, there have been literally thousands of space ships seen over every country in the world. They have been tracked many times on radar screens. They have been seen visually from both the ground and the air. They have been photographed. They have been filmed.

Furthermore, many contacts have taken place between the

occupants of the space ships and selected people on this earth. The best known of these contacts is that of George Adamski. This now famous meeting with a man from another world took place at Desert Centre, California on November 20, 1952, and was fully described in the best selling book "Flying Saucers have Landed" by Desmond Leslie and George Adamski. There were six witnesses to the event, including Dr. George Hunt Willliamson who is lecturing in England this month.

Some startling new evidence has just come to light concerning this historic encounter. Those who read the book will recall how it was stated on p.210 that several planes, including a B36, had circled over the vicinity at the time. Flying Saucer Review, which I have the honour to edit, now has on file photostat copies of two letters written by the U. S. Air Technical Intelligence Centre (ATIC) to one of our readers. The first letter, dated August 3, 1956, states : "In response to your letter of July 18, 1956, we are enclosing a summary of Project Bluebook Special Report No. 14 which was released in October, 1955. The full report statistically covers all reports up to that date, **including a report by an Air Force pilot on November 20, 1958, from the general Vicinity of Desert Centre, California....**

Our reader then wrote for further information as to what was actually in that very important UFO report, only to be told that it was not Air Force policy to disclose the contents of UFO reports.

However, the above information is the first time that the US Air Force has ever disclosed that it did see something on that day at Desert Centre. And it certainly is another big step towards confirming once and for all that famous meeting.

There have been many other contacts between those of other worlds and earthlings, including many that have not hitherto been published. Some are undoubtedly hoaxes, but the majority have a certain similar pattern running through them. The time is coming when it will be realized that Man extends throughout the Universe, and that we have brothers on many a far-flung galaxy. Man in the human form is universal, and this is but one of the many forms we take on our march towards perfection.

Although the number of people who are taking flying saucers seriously is growing very fast, millons still either do not know of these space craft in our skies or still treat the subject flippantly. This state of affairs is chiefly due to the lack of official acknowledgment of our space visitors from Government level.

In 1953 a scientific panel met at the request of the U. S. Government. They stated in their findings, dated January 17,1953, that the saucers were not hostile. The report was not released until April 9, 1958, by the U. S. Air Force. If the space visitors are friendly, then why do not the authorities tell us about them officially? According to the above information, they have known for five years that they are not hostile, so why could not the authorities have spent that time educating public opinion to the concept of space visitors, if they were afraid of breaking the news of their existence at once? All that has happened is that the public have had an extra large dose of horror films, dealing with invasions by Martians armed with death rays. These terrifying science fiction films continue to be our form of education.

Space ships are of friendly intent towards us. They have been noted in our skies from the earliest times There are records of them in the Vedas (they were called Vimans then); they were known in ancient Egypt; the American Indians tell of them; there are records of them in the Bible; there are numerous references to them in the journals of learned societies in the nineteenth century. During all this time the space ships have never harmed us.

(9)

The coming of the space ships in increasing numbers at this critical period of our history may have the most tremendous implications for mankind and for the future of our world.

Now too, that we are taking the initial steps towards journeying into outer space, people everywhere are fast becoming more space-conscious, and our space visitors are also intensifying their visits to us. These two facts may be inter-related.

Yes, it is indeed a comforting thought to realize that Man on earth is not alone in the Universe. We have friends and neighbours in space.

THE DAWN OF A NEW AGE

J. S. Yajnik, Banaras Hindu University.

The tremendous strides which science has made in recent times have culminated in releasing nuclear energy and sending up artificial moons to circle round the earth. These achievements inspire hope that within measurable time space stations may be established and interplanetary communication may become a possibility, and ultimately the dream of exploring the cosmos may be realized

The credit for these achievements goes to the combined efforts and technical skill of a number of scientists, who, liberally encouraged and helped by their governments, made their individual contributions at different stages and thus heralded the age of nuclear energy. But this is only a prelude to a more marvellous age of space travel.

On two engrossing problems depends the fate of the world and the future of mankind. However gratifying the progress made in the realm of science may have been, it has now brought the world to the brink of utter ruin if a single false step is taken. The mounting tension among the Great Powers, armed with nuclear weapons, may at any time result in a global war, the consequences of which are too appalling to imagine. The face of the earth would be distorted out of shape ; the human race would be wiped away, and the survivors, if any, would be reduced to the most primitive conditions of living, civilization and science becoming things of the past.

To avert such a dire calamity and colossal devastation is the most important function of the United Nations Organization. It has to strive succesfully for the universal acceptance of the ideal of ONE World; otherwise one spark will carry man to his inevitable doom.

WE ARE NOT ALONE IN THE UNIVERSE

(11)

The other problem equally fraught with the gravest consequences is of interplanetary communication, of space ships and flying saucers, and man's dream of space conquest. The UNO must address itself to this problem also on a worldwide basis, so that the conquest of space by one country may not become a menace or source of terror to the other countries. And for this it is necessary that the UNO should exercise control over the development of the elemental atomic energy and its uses for humanity. This will not only ensure its use only for beneficial purposes but help in its speedy development by the joint and co-operative effort of the world scientists under the auspices of the UNO.

It is too late in the day now to deny the existence of flying objects from outer space. Attempts to explain them away have, to say the least, proved simply puerile. Innumerable sightings by hundreds of observers the world over, and their authentic evidence are so overwhelming that even the mighty governments can no more mislead the people or conceal the obvious facts. Political reasons may have some justification for avoiding panic among the people but the frequency with which the unidentified foreign objects have been appearing leave no room for doubt in the minds of reasonable persons that the denizens of other planets have already achieved what our scientists are only striving for and in which they are still in the initial stages.

There is no remedy for the attitude of cynical scepticism. Those who are determined to shut their eyes to the obvious can never be convinced. In the highest quarters the reality of these objects and their spatial origin is admitted. There is now abundance of literature on the subject, press reports and current journals, the perusal of which will convince any inquirer who cares to know the truth. The massed evidence of the flying saucers and space ships has been supported by photographs and the testimony of observers whose veracity cannot be doubted.

(12)

For ages man believed that the earth was the centre of the universe and that he was at the top of the created beings. Entertaining such notions about his own superiority and his domain it is naturally difficult for him to admit readily a lower position for himself and for the earth in the solar system. Now he has to realize the fact that he is not the king of the universe. He did not believe that the planets or stars had any living beings. The scientist also, till the other day, proclaimed that the moon and Mars could not sustain life as known upon the earth. It is no easy matter to dislodge such beliefs held since the dawn of civilization. And references to space flights and communication with the planets in ancient lore have always been treated as figments of imagination. Man will have to give up his unscientific notions and sacrifice his ego when accepting the latest discoveries made by the scientist and the astronomer. In the Middle Ages the defiance of the prevailing faith and challenge to superstition meant torture and death, but in the present age of science one can smother truth and refuse to accept an established fact with impunity. At least this has been the case with the flying saucers, the truth about which has been deliberately suppressed by governments and very high officials. There is ample evidence to show that there is a conspiracy of silence in the United States Government and crude attempts are made to conceal true facts from the public.

From the innumerable observations recorded by laymen, scientists and astronomers, some important features of space ships and flying saucers have been definitely laid down. In shape and form they are entirely different from all man-made flying machines. Space ships are of a very big size and contain in them smaller flying saucers—say half a. dozen. The mother-ship can stay in the sky steady and motionless, while the saucers come down near or upon the earth, to rise again and to be taken in by the mother-ship. Almost always they are silent, though at times attaining the tremendous speed of 25,000 miles per hour in our atmosphere, and yet remaining unburnt by the friction. In the outer space above the atmosphere they may possibly attain the speed of light—1,86,000 miles per second. They are undoubtedly controlled by intelligent beings who have achieved mechanical perfection for their craft yet unknown to man. Not only is the suppression of sound vibrations made possible, but they are converted into light vibrations of different colours. The Tibetan Yogis are said to know the secret of converting sound into light which they use when required in their dark caves. The motive power of the space ships is not the same as that used by man-made craft. It is probable that they use electro-magnetic power or the inexhaustible energy of the cosmic rays. No man can survive at the tremendous speed of these weird machines, especia-ly when they take sudden and sharp turns maintaining uniform speed. It seems that the intelligent operators of the space ships command unlimited power and know how to convert atomic energy directly into electricity and have discovered the secret of freedom from gravitational attraction.

All these features conclusively prove that the luminous flying saucers cruising at fantastic speeds come from the outer space and are piloted by beings of superior intelligence who have acquired mastery over the forces of nature yet unknown to man. From this it naturally follows that some of the planets are inhabited by thinking, intelligent beings more advanced than man. There is every probability that there are distant worlds inhabited by beings whose knowledge and attainments are beyond our wildest dreams.

Not only do the flying saucers prove that some of the planets are inhabited, but independent testimony of some astronomers supports this fact. After making thousands of observations, and after mapping about 700 canals, Lowell, a distinguished astronomer, announced: "Mars is inhabited. We have absolute proof" Changes on its surface have been noticed which indicate that they are artificial and made by intelligent beings. Like our earth, other planets can also evolve life if conditions are congenial. And if life is evolved, later mind must also evolve. Different atmospheres and other varying factors may evolve forms and features of beings different from those of men.

Astronomers have been keenly watching mysterious activities on the surface of the moon. Scientists tell us that there is no atmosphere there, and consequently no life can exist there. Extremes of temperature, too, cannot allow any living creature to survive. But these surmises are based upon the conditions required by man for his existence. There may be life there of some kind to which the physical conditions are congenial. In recent times dome-like structures and a big bridge have appeared on the surface. So there may be a moon race or a base may have been formed there by the inhabitants of Mars or some other planet. If Russians claim to reach the moon within twenty years, the more advanced denizens of some planets may be already there by their superior scientific knowledge.

Flying saucers have not only appeared in our skies but landed too. George Adamski has had the unique good fortune of not only photographing a flying saucer but also meeting an occupant of it who came from Venus and seeing the inside of a space ship. Relating his extraordinary experience, he and his companions swore an affidavit before a notary public. His books **Flying Saucers have landed** and **Inside the Space Ships** are convincing and are of absorbing interest. Inhabitants of Saturn, Venus and Mars have been repoted to have landed and safely returned to their respective planets.

The question is: Why do they come? We do not know and speculate that they come on pleasure trips with a feeling of triumph on their achievements. They are friendly and desire contact with us. They warn us that the nuclear explosions here are fraught with tragic possibilities not only to our earth but also to the entire solar system. If our world is destroyed, the rhythmic movements of the solar system are bound to be affected. They desire to help us in our effort to conquer space and give us the advantage of their superior knowledge, and draw us closer to them. At present there is only one-way traffic; with their help it can become a two-way one. The visitors from outer space are not hostile; this is proved by the fact that they have done nothing wrong to anybody. Two tragic accidents are said to have happened. In the one case an aeroplane pursued a flying saucer and went dangerously near it and was destroyed on account of its close proximity by some ray or emanation from the saucer. But it was not an intentional hostile act. In the other case the pursuers were perhaps kidnapped by the occupants of the flying saucer and safely carried to some other planet. There was absolutely no trace of the pursuing aeroplane or its remnants.

Care has to be taken that no flying saucer is fired upon, lest it should provoke retaliation. It seems that the visitors are afraid that men here may damage their machine, making their return flight impossible or capture the visitors and ill-treat them. It is conceivable that mass landings will take place when peace prevails on earth and there is no danger of a global war.

Thus we see that the UNO has a double role to play, firstly, to establish peace here and eliminate the fear of war, and secondly, to organize world opinion for a friendly attitude towards the visitors from outer space and ensure their safety.

It may safely be predicted that the visitors, if properly welcomed and treated with due consideration, may show us the way to peace and prosperity never known before, and usher us into a Golden Age in which the conquest of space will become a reality.

THE GREATEST EVENT OF THE PRESENT CENTURY

S. K. Maitra, Banaras Hindu University.

Undoubtedly the greatest event of the present century, if not of all centuries, is the appearance of spacecraft from other worlds. It far eclipses every other event in importance and in its possibilities for the human race. In fact, it is not possible to exaggerate its significance for us human beings, as it heralds the advent of a New Age.

Yes, it heralds a New Age which will completely transform our present human civilization. So revolutionary will be the changes that will come with it in the structure of our human society, that it is impossible for us to envisage them. We can only say that it will cause such a radical transformation of the conditions of our life as has never been witnessed in our history.

For it will transform us from our present position as Earthly Men into Cosmic Men. This transformation is a necessity for us if we are to survive. Our present position, thanks to the hydrogen bomb and the nuclear tests and worldwide tension, has become so bad and is deteriorating so fast, that unless some radical change occurs, we are doomed. The hydrogen bomb and the nuclear tests are a warning to us that unless we mend our ways thoroughly, the entire human race is going to be exterminated.

But the great Indian sage and philosopher Sri Aurobindo has emphatically declared that the human race is destined not to die. The present gloomy conditions are, as he has clearly pointed out, only an indication that one stage of man's evolution is going to end in order to usher in another and a higher stage. They are to be looked upon as the birthpangs of a New Age. It is necessary that we should with all our mind and all our soul welcome these signs which are proclaiming the advent of a far more glorious age than the present one.

The strange spacecraft that have been seen by thousands of people and in thousand different places and some of which have also been seen to land, carry with them the message of our deliverance. They tell us that our destiny is not to remain earth-bound, that there are vaster worlds beyond our own, of which we are also citizens and where we are destined to play our part. And it is only when we realize our cosmic self that we can fulfil our destiny. Not only so, but even our earthly problems we can only solve when we rise to the cosmic level, just as it is only when we ascend the top of a mountain that we can see clearly everything in the valley, which we cannot do when we are ourselves in it.

But unfortunately, the whole machinery of practically all the Governments on our planet is employed to hide from us these signs of the dawning of a new Age which will deliver us from the evils of the present one. What a colossal folly! What a terrible perversity! It is also extremely regrettable that our men of science have not so far protested against this policy of the Governments. Not only have they not protested, but they have in many cases taken an active part in this campaign of suppression of news relating to these strange spacecraft. There are, of course, notable exceptions. All honour to them for their courageous stand against their own Governments and also against their own colleagues. But unfortunately, their number is very small, compared with that of those who are helping their Governments in their hush-hush policy. The general public also, and especially, our legislators, the chosen representatives of our people in the legislative bodies, have also a duty to perform in this matter, which, I regret to say they have so far neglected. If they with one voice had demanded that all facts in the possession of their respective Governments should be made public, no Government on earth could have ignored such a demand.

As an example of how the public are systematically deluded by the authorities about the nature of the strange spacecraft that are seen in our skies, may be mentioned the answer given by the Under-Secretary of State for Air in the British House of Commons, as recorded in the current (July-August) number of "Flying Saucer Review", when a member asked the Government about the number and nature of the strange objects that had been seen moving in the sky by so many people at so many different places. I quote below *verbatim* the account as given in this number of this Review.

"On June 10 Mr. Chetwynd asked a question in the House of of Commons : "How many instances of unidentified flying objects had been reported on by the defence services of the United Kingdom during the last 12 months, and what steps were taken to co-ordinate such observations ?"

"Mr. Charles I. Orr-Ewing, Under-Secretary of State for Air, replied, "Reports of 54 unidentified flying objects have been received in the last 12 months. Such co-ordination as is necessary is undertaken by the Air Ministry. Most of the objects turn out to be meteors, balloons or aircraft. Satellites have also accounted for a number of recent reports".

I quote also the remarks of the Editor of this Review on this answer of the British Minister, which I fully endorse :

"What an absurd and vague reply ! As Captain Ferreira would say, 'Don't give me that old routine.' (See "Air Force Pilots spend 40 minutes with Saucers"—last issue.) The first point to notice is that they have had only 54 reports in the last 12 months. Flying Saucer Review gets that in a couple of weeks or less. The second point shows that the answer is incomplete and useless. Mr. Orr-Ewing says "most of the objects" turn out to be ballooney. If, say, only 5 objects out of 54 turned out to be unknown, then Mr. Chetwynd's question is more than justified. As it is, the Under-Secretary's answer tells us nothing. This, of course, is what the Government intended to do".

There have been other similar instances where British Ministers have given such vague and misleading answers to questions concerning flying saucers put to them by members. One such occurred on the 20th March 1957, when, in reply to the question put by Mr. Leavey, relating to the strange spacecraft seen at Wardle, near Rochdale, Lancashire, the British Under-Secretary for War described them as toy balloons released by a laundry mechanic ! The whole incident has been described in great detail in "Flying Saucer Review" for May-June 1957 under the title "The Wardle Mystery".

But worse things than these have happened in America, where a man was at first tortured in a police station and later sent to a mental hospital for refusing to recant his statement, that not only had he seen a flying saucer but had seen its crew and had a joy ride in it. A full report of this case is given in "Flying Saucer Review" for May-June 1958 and a summary of it has appeared in the current (July-August) number of this Review.

But why all this secrecy ? Why this desperate attempt to hide the fact that spacecraft from other worlds have come and are still coming in large numbers to our planet ? Is it to conceal the fact that there are beings more advanced than ourselves in this universe ? But why should we feel ashamed at this ? Is it not the part of wisdom to acknowledge this fact and try to establish contact with these superior beings who are coming from other worlds ?

(20)

The press in our country also, I am sorry to say, seems to have joined this conspiracy of silence. There is practically a complete blackout of all news concerning these strange objects that are seen in our skies.

It is high time that steps were taken to stop this. There should be ufological *conferences in every country for not only collecting information about these strange spacecraft but also devising ways and means of establishing contact with them. To these conferences not only scientists and technicians but persons in other walks of life should be invited. There should also be held an International Ufological Congress at some central place, like New Delhi or London or Washington. One of the objects of such a Congress will be to establish an International Ufological Institute to make researches on all matters connected with ufology, such as the possibility of controlling gravity, the method of propulsion of flying saucers and space ships, possibility of communicating with our sister planets, etc. An attempt should also be made to request the UNO to provide the necessary funds for such an Institute, for there can be no doubt that such an Institute is a fit object for receiving financial assistance from the UNO. If, however, the UNO refuses to give financial assistance, then efforts will have to be made to get the necessary funds from other organizations.

These are some of the suggestions that occur to me for bringing the significance of the great event which at present passes almost unnoticed, to an increasingly large number of people on our globe, and thus slowly but surely removing the scepticism concerning it which is still prevalent and which is one of the saddest features of our life at present.

There is another aspect of this matter. If we show an increasing eagerness to contact the flying saucers and their crew, they, on their part, will be more eager than they are at present to meet us, and thus we may hope to accelerate the advent of that Great Day when contact with our sister planets and also with the stellar world will be as easy as contact with different parts of our globe is at the present moment.

---

* The word *Ufology* means the science relating to unidentified flying objects.

UNIDENTIFIED FLYING OBJECTS

Dr. S. S. Banerjee,
Engineering College, Banaras Hindu University

From the innumerable records of sightings of the flying saucers or the unidentified flying objects (U. F. O.), it is now almost convincing that the interplanetary transport has been made possible by the inhabitants of some other planet like Venus or others. If we have to believe the reports, there have been instances when flying saucers have landed on our planet and their occupants have also been seen to disembark and had personal contacts with a few rare observers. The Venusians, if we may call them, have been described as almost similar to the inhabitants of our planet with difference in minor details, and they could speak some European language not unknown in our globe.

It is therefore imperative that more attention should now be devoted by the scientists and engineers of all countries to investigate the possibility of such interplanetary flights and understand the principle and mechanism of such flying objects which are reported to attain tremendous velocity much higher than the velocity of light in the inter-planetary space. Flying Saucer Review from England has published ample instances of sightings of such objects and has also published extracts of talks regarding the theory of flight as explained by the Captain of a flying saucer. Photographs have also been taken of such flying objects by George Adamski in U. S. A.

Before we enter into its theory it may be mentioned that the shape of the flying saucer, as described by the various observers from different parts of the globe, is the same, and it looks like a big round helmet about 13 to 14 ft. in diameter at the bottom and a dome of about 10 to 12 ft. high. It has portholes near the top of the dome and it spins when it travels in space. The remarkable feature is that it attains a very high velocity within a very short time and can take turn even at right angles to its original direction of motion at high speed.

The easy escape of these flying objects from the gravitational field of one planet evidently arouses the greatest interest and warrants the necessity of deeper probe into the matter. This definitely requires the revision of the entire conception of the interplanetary motion, an outline of which is given below as collected from the reports.

According to the extra-terrestrial scientists the sun is not assumed to be the centre of the planetary system, and the interplanetary force is not due to gravity but due to the attraction of several magnetic fields. For instance, it is assumed that there is an immense primary magnetic field in the Milky Way within which there are several secondary fields. Such fields in the galaxy have no doubt been calculated by Chandrashekhar and Fermi but they are of a very small order. The movements of the planets are controlled by this magnetic field or the magnetic centre which they call 'point zero'. It is further stated that the solar light exerts a pressure on the planets which is equivalent to a repulsive force. Thus the essence of the theory is that the pressure exerted by the light from the sun and the force of attraction due to the magnetic field balance each other.

The theory necessarily requires an atmosphere surrounding the earth at the periphery of which the force is exerted by the solar light, which also avoids the effect of blanketing the sun due to the weather conditions in the lower atmosphere. The revolution of the earth is, however, the result of the speed of rotation and the atmosphere of the earth which gives a support on which the earth revolves. They have calculated the ethereal radius of the earth from the speed of rotation and revolution, and the terrestrial radius. Thus it has been shown that the radius of the gaseous mass surrounding the earth is 407, 200 kms. Subtracting the terrestrial radius from this, one gets the ethereal radius as 400, 822 kms. Thus the effective diameter of the earth for calculating the magnetic field has been found to be 814, 400 kms.

According to this theory a large planet will be further away from the sun. It has been thus shown that in the case of Jupiter, the density of which is low but has a larger diameter than the earth, it is more repelled than attracted. According to the usual gravitational law, Jupiter which has a volume 1330 times greater than that of the earth and which is 331 times heavier than the earth, should be closer to the sun than the earth, whereas on the contrary, it is further away from the sun. This proves the validity of the extra-terrestrial theory of the movement of the planets.

This theory of the magnetic field has been applied in the case of interplanetary flights Mention has also been made that temperature plays an important part in controlling the magnetic field which is also evidenced by the different colours of the saucer, while taking off or changing its speed, from blue to yellow and red. Thus it appears that the principle of flight of space ships is likely to depend on a theory far remote from the conventional gravitational theory which is worthy of development as early as possible. The above theory therefore does require thorough investigation, as the importance of the problem lies not only in acquiring the knowledge of the fundamental principles of the interplanetary system, but also in the fact that the solution of it may bring lasting peace to the world.

UFOS—A GAME FOR ABSTRACTIONS: A BRIEF AND DIDACTIC DISCUSSION

J. Escobar Faria,
Editor, "UFO CRITICAL BULLETIN", Sao Paulo, Brazil

When something new under study becomes an abstract subject, it is normal that it should pass into another category. So is it with UFOs.

At present we have all pieces of the game, but if we put them in their due places, even then we do not get a clear picture. This is why the UFO problem has changed its category—from a reality in the skies to a very abstraction in our minds.

Our reality, the most factual reality, indeed does not fit in with that of the UFOs just because all pieces of such concreteness do not give any answer to the question. What are the UFOs? Are they man-made devices? No, absolutely they are not. Why? Because we earthians cannot emulate in any way the UFOs' performances. Yet we never can say that they are from other planets. Why? Because we have no evidence. We can only theorize and speculate. Personally this writer believes that the UFOs are coming from other worlds more highly advanced in science and technology. But if one asks for a proof, the same writer will be absolutely silent. He possesses indeed a logical background, but he does not possess a proof. Even the powerful USAF does not possess such a proof. Thus, when the writer discusses the matter, surely he does nothing more than a battle of ideas without any scientific or technical supporting evidence. All are abstractions.

So far the UFOs are still an abstract category for us. These elusive contraptions have become themselves a subject for abstract studies, like, for instance, astronomy. We may see stars, measure them, analyze them, etc. But we do not know precisely what stars factually are at all. We know about them through mathematical and spectroscopic measurements (through photos by telescopes) **only**. So is it with UFOs. We can study their amazing performances in the sky, their manoeuvres, colours, flights, etc. We can even establish certain definite patterns for them (as astrophysicists do for heavenly bodies). But we do not **know what** UFOs are, just as astrophysicists do not know what stars are, too. An astrophysicist, like Dr. Menzel, of course, might say, "What you are saying is nonsense. I, Dr. Menzel, do say that I **know** what stars are". Well, then, what about an anti-star ? An anti-planet ? An anti-electron ? And so on. Science knows that when a proton collides against an anti-proton (or an electron against an anti-electron, etc.), there occurs a microcosmic explosion delivering energy. Are there anti-stars, anti-planets, anti-beings, and...an ANTI-LIFE ? Some scientists have speculated about them. Surely, astrophysicists do not know what stars are.

All talk about UFOs is therefore nothing more than a speculation, and speculations do not reach a known reality, having a **definite** meaning ; rather they fall into a maze of mental games.

What, then, can this writer say finally ? Nothing more than this. Be humble, you **ufologists**, before things from the UNKNOWN. Be like Socrates, and duplicate the old dictum : **What I know is just this, that I know absolutely nothing.**

Published by
S. K. Maitra
Quarters No. D/8.
Banaras Hindu University.

Printed at the Uttara Press,
Bhelupura, Varanasi.

Further reading

George Adamski – The facts in context
A free online resource, this website documents the scope of Adamski's mission, the impact of his work, and the relevance of his teaching. It also features a unique illustrated biographical timeline, and an exposé of the most common misrepresentations of Adamski's work and motives. Visit: www-the-adamski-case.nl.

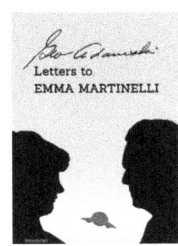

George Adamski – Letters to Emma Martinelli
Published in full for the first time, George Adamski's letters to his student Emma Martinelli, written between 1950 and 1952, shed light on this pivotal phase in his mission, and underscore the central thread of his teaching about the Oneness and universality of Life. The introduction by Gerard Aartsen provides the historical context in which these letters were written, challenges many of the commonly-held beliefs of critics and detractors, and casts a new and unexpected light on matters that were long considered foregone conclusions by most other writers.
BGA Publications 2022. Paperback, 108 pages. ISBN: 978-90-830336-2-4.

The Sea of Consciousness, feat. The Invisible Ocean
The Sea of Consciousness includes the integral text of George Adamski's lost debut *The Invisible Ocean*, two previously unpublished articles and a special clippings section documenting and demystifying his time with the Royal Order of Tibet. In three separate essays, researcher Gerard Aartsen outlines how
– Adamski's philosophy is now being confirmed by 21st century science;
– historical facts expose the long-standing false allegations against Adamski; and
– science is edging ever closer to the recognition that the manifestation of life may not be limited to our carbon-based reality.
BGA Publications 2019. Paperback, 118 pages. ISBN: 978-90-9031695-6.

UFOs and the Pioneers of Oneness
This groundbreaking inquiry into the reality of extraterrestrial visitors brings an entirely new understanding of the nature of life on our planet and in Cosmos itself, devoid of mysticism, sensationalism or superficiality. The author's synthesis of findings from systems science, quantum research, the wisdom teachings and ET contact experiences reveals how today's perilous tensions are actually the birth pangs of a new sense of oneness, and shows that our problems arise from humanity's struggle to manifest an underlying essential interconnectedness.
BGA Publications, 2020. Paperback edition 2022, 276 pages. ISBN: 978-90-830336-1-7.

About the author

Gerard Aartsen worked as a translator before he became a teacher trainer at the Amsterdam University of Applied Sciences School of Education in 2001. As a student of the Ageless Wisdom teaching, his interest in George Adamski's philosophy was prompted after reading *Wisdom of the Masters of the Far East* and *Inside the Space Ships*.

His first book, *George Adamski – A Herald for the Space Brothers* (2010), was the first to attempt an integral look at Adamski's philosophy, which he then correlated with the accounts of other contactees of the 1950s in his following books, published in 2011, 2015, 2016 and 2020. Several of these were also published in Dutch, French, Japanese, Spanish, German and Finnish.

After rediscovering and republishing Adamski's lost debut *The Invisible Ocean* in 2019, that same year Gerard published The Adamski Case website (*George Adamski – The facts in context*), that has become the go-to online source for fact- and evidence-based information about Adamski's life, mission and teaching.

Early 2022 he published Adamski's letters to Emma Martinelli, a member of the San Francisco Interplanetary Club, written between 1950 and 1952, with an enlightening introduction and annotations.

In *The Adamski Book of UFO/UAP Disclosure*, Gerard brings together all the fundamentals of the UFO phenomenon as presented by George Adamski that have been confirmed by relevant authoritative sources, providing a comprehensive overview of the information about the extraterrestrial presence on Earth that has been disclosed so far.

For more information: www.bgapublications.nl

www.ingramcontent.com/pod-product-compliance
Lightning Source LLC
LaVergne TN
LVHW070601070526
838199LV00011B/458